Community Approaches

TO Feral Cats

D1531010

PROBLEMS,

ALTERNATIVES, &

RECOMMENDATIONS

by Margaret R. Slater

Humane Society Press
an affiliate of

THE HUMANE SOCIETY
OF THE UNITED STATES.

First edition
ISBN 0-9658942-5-8

Library of Congress Cataloging-in-Publication Data

Slater, Margaret R.
  Community approaches to feral cats: problems, alternatives,
and recommendations / by Margaret R. Slater.
      p. cm.
Includes bibliographical references and index.
  ISBN 0-9658942-5-8
1. Feral cats.   2. Feral cats—Control.   3. Feral cats—United States.
4. Feral cats—Control—United States.   I. Title.
  SF450+

                                              2002002359
Printed in the United States of America

Humane Society Press
An affiliate of The Humane Society of the United States
2100 L Street, NW
Washington, DC 20037

Margaret R. Slater, D.V.M., Ph.D., is associate professor of epidemiology in the departments of Veterinary Anatomy and Public Health and Small Animal Medicine and Surgery in the College of Veterinary Medicine at Texas A&M University in College Station, Texas.

Acknowledgments

I would like to thank Martha Armstrong and Leslie Sinclair, D.V.M., for their invaluable assistance with the logistics and contacts for my feral cat sabbatical project, from which this book sprang. I'd also like to thank The Humane Society of the United States for its financial support and The HSUS's Geoffrey L. Handy and Deborah J. Salem for their time and effort in making the book as good as it could possibly be.

I would like to acknowledge my debt to my cat, Pinwheel, for providing me with a recent exposure to different definitions of ownership. When a friend recognized Pinwheel as a neighbor's cat and told his former owner of his whereabouts, the owner was unconcerned to learn that he had been in the shelter, unclaimed, for five days prior to his adoption.

I particularly appreciate the time, knowledge, opinions, and data shared with me by many people around the country and my experiences with the many felines who gave me more insight into the life of feral (and not-so-feral) cats.

Other Books in the Humane Society Press Public Policy Series

The Use of Animals in Higher Education
by Jonathan Balcombe, Ph.D.

The State of the Animals: 2001
edited by Deborah J. Salem and Andrew N. Rowan

Animal Control Management: A Guide for Local Governments
by Geoffrey L. Handy
(published by the International City/County Management Association)

This book is intended to provide useful information regarding feral cats; however, a word of warning is in order. Feral cats sometimes behave unpredictibly, especially when they are under stress. Caring for a feral cat inevitably involves some risk of injury to the cat, to other animals, to persons, or to property. Feral cats sometimes have hidden health or psychological problems that may cause them to react unfavorably to treatment that would otherwise be considered proper. The information provided in this book is not intended to substitute for veterinary, legal, or other professional advice. Laws regarding the treatment and disposition of animals vary from place to place, and lobbying and other forms of activism are regulated or may otherwise result in legal consequences.

The information in this book should be used with caution and in accordance with all state and local animal control laws and regulations; you must rely on your own judgment in using this book or seek professional advice. Your use of this book expressly indicates your assumption of risk of injury or other consequences resulting from interacting with animals or using any products or procedures mentioned in this book. Neither the author nor The Humane Society of the United States assumes any liability for any injury to persons or property that may result from the use of this book.

The views expressed by the author do not necessarily reflect the views of The Humane Society of the United States.

Contents

Foreword

All domestic cats deserve loving, permanent homes with responsible caregivers who keep them safely confined and meet their special needs.

This is a belief that I hold close. It is a view shared by millions of cat lovers around the world. It is the published opinion of The Humane Society of the United States (HSUS). And yet, although more than 60 million cats have gently clawed their way into our homes and hearts, tens of millions more cats subsist outside of homes—abandoned, stray, or feral.

These free-roaming cats elude simple categorization, but the feral cat most embodies the failure of humans to take full responsibility for the animals they domesticated thousands of years ago. Feral cats, one or more generations removed from a happy home and too unsocialized to be placed in a home, can survive on their own. But it cannot be said that they thrive.

Almost every community has feral cats. These cats may be left alone—by ignoring them, tolerating them, or wanting to do something but looking the other way out of helplessness or ignorance—or they may be removed or managed in some way. "Managing" feral cat colonies usually means humanely trapping the cats, having them spayed or neutered and vaccinated, and then releasing them.

As with so many issues in animal protection, philosophy and pragmatism collide when considering the best options for feral cats. After all, to trap feral cats humanely only to return them to the situation from which they came is to institutionalize a system in which some cats are likely to meet a bad end. Even the sterilized, vaccinated cat living on an isolated parcel of land in a temperate climate and being fed by the most dedicated caregiver is susceptible to a range of threats that the well-cared-for indoor cat will never face. No colony, no matter how well maintained, can protect cats from accidental or intentional injury or death, abuse, or diseases that cannot be prevented by vaccination. And, of course, the maintenance of any colony means tolerating the continued predation by cats on a variety of wildlife, both winged and furred.

As Margaret Slater characterizes it, active feral cat colony management is an interim solution, one that recognizes that the only unacceptable option is to do nothing. We cannot let cats continue to breed and suffer, leaving each successive generation of felines to live on the fringes of human existence facing shortened—and in many cases painful—lives. Sadly, that is what continues to happen in many communities where a void of knowledge, leadership, resources, and consensus leaves free-roaming cats with nary an ounce of the human protection that they need and deserve.

I hope that this book will help fill that void. Cats are mysterious to some, but the options for dealing with them should not be. Fortunately, Margaret Slater has succeeded in demystifying and defining the issues that surround feral and other free-roaming cats. Viewing these issues through the lenses of epidemiology and veterinary medicine, Slater presents and evaluates a variety of options for managing feral cat colonies, both practiced and theoretical, to inform policymakers, legislators, animal advocates, and other interested parties. Slater adds her voice to the chorus of concerned feral cat caregivers and other local activists—the field marshals of cat advocacy—who have chosen to take responsibility for these animals.

It is that message—that cats are not wild animals, but our responsibility—that resonates throughout this book. Responsibility begets obligation, which begets initiative, which begets action. Only through action, taken community by community, will we achieve a world in which every domestic cat gets the loving, safe, and permanent home that she deserves.

Martha C. Armstrong
Senior Vice President, Companion Animals and Equine Protection
The Humane Society of the United States

Introduction

1.1. Scope of This Monograph

This book is the culmination of a research project undertaken by the author and funded by The HSUS to analyze and review existing data on feral cat management and control, develop standard definitions and data collection schemes, and create a set of proposed research needs to address unanswered questions regarding the feral cat problem.

This book has been created to fill many of the gaps in stakeholders' knowledge of feral cats and how best to deal with them. These gaps are evident in the tremendous variation in communities' responses to the "feral cat problem"—from doing nothing to implementing broad-based feral cat colony management programs designed to "manage" colonies into extinction.

Whether a community addresses the problem of feral cats or not, it still has the problem. For the estimated tens of millions of free-roaming domestic cats considered to be feral, the problem is often one of premature death and some degree of suffering prior to death. Feral cats cause many concerns, including public health concerns, but the cats' suffering is the ultimate concern of The HSUS and the primary reason that The HSUS has published this book. By informing policymakers and other stakeholders about feral cat-related problems and solutions, The HSUS hopes to engage them to take enlightened, effective action.

Appendices include materials useful to humane societies, feral cat care-takers, and veterinarians, as well as sample legislative approaches and detailed case studies that illustrate approaches to active management of feral cat colonies.

Overview

1.1 Defining the Problem

The mere mention of feral cats creates a storm of emotion and controversy for many people. Where do feral cats come from? What should be done about them? What is best for them? Who is responsible for them? Although the cats themselves often are at the center of the storm, feral cats are a "people problem." They are the offspring of outdoor, intact cats—owned or abandoned. They are on farms and in cities, suburbs, and wilderness areas. They can be found near schools, restaurants, hospitals, barns, apartments, and abandoned buildings—anywhere there is adequate food and shelter (Mahlow and Slater 1996). Some people feed them, others provide veterinary care; some feel sorry for them but do nothing, others that believe they should be removed and destroyed. Even the veterinary profession is divided on how to view feral cats, as reflected in conflicting and often emotional letters in the *Journal of the American Veterinary Medical Association* (Hughes 1993; DeBrito and Doffermyre 1994; Heerens 1994; Heerens 1996; Gross et al. 1996; McGrath 1996; Patronek 1996). These letters were responses to an article on controlling feral cats through neuter and release (Zaunbrecher and Smith 1993) and a later American Veterinary Medical Association (AVMA) report on cat welfare and overpopulation (Kahler 1996).

What is a "feral" cat? For this book, any cat who is too poorly socialized to be handled (and therefore must be trapped or sedated for examination) and who cannot be placed into a typical pet home is *feral*. Any cat who is not confined to a house or another enclosure is *free-roaming*. Feral cats are a subpopulation of free-roaming cats. Free-roaming cats generally cause whatever cat-related problems exist in a given area, yet feral cats, specifically, are usually blamed for such problems. (An *abandoned* cat is one who may be tame but does not currently have an owner and is free-roaming. *Stray cats* are currently or recently owned cats who may be lost from their homes. They are usually well socialized initially but over time may become feral.) This book focuses on feral cats and free-roaming cats without a responsible owner or caretaker.

At the heart of the conflict about how to treat feral cats is the need to address complaints and concerns that arise from their existence. This need is particularly compelling for animal care and control agencies and humane societies. Historically, stray and feral cats were trapped and euthanized. Such an approach was believed to be the kindest solution for a homeless cat and is still the approach used in many parts of the country, especially where rabies is a problem or where public interest in cats is low. But this approach may not be an effective—or tolerable—solution.

The complexity of this issue is apparent in the different views among wildlife and bird enthusiasts, cat owners, the general public, and other constituencies (Patronek 1998). Any free-roaming cat may hunt wildlife, but feral cats are often the highest-profile subgroup in the community that does so. The conflict typically involves people of three different viewpoints.

The first point of view is that some free-roaming cats kill many birds and other wildlife. Since cats are domestic animals and should be under the care and control of people, they should not be permitted to hunt birds and wildlife. According to this viewpoint, allowing cats to kill wildlife places more value on the cats' lives than on the lives of the animals they hunt.

The second view is that, putting the relative value of life aside, free-roaming cats may have a negative impact on biodiversity and on endangered species. There is a sizable literature on the impact of cats on wildlife, but most of the work has been done in island ecosystems that are not representative of much of the United States. Several of the most commonly cited studies have been quoted out of context or the results extrapolated inappropriately (Patronek 1998). The limited data available do not support the argument that cats are the primary cause of species destruction on the mainland of the United States, especially in urban environments. In some locations, however, cats may constitute an additional pressure on already threatened wildlife populations.

The third perspective is that cats are not a natural part of the ecosystem, particularly those cats who are fed by people. These cats, because they are well fed, are better able to hunt—and do so for recreation rather than sustenance. They, therefore, do not fit into the normal patterns of a wild habitat and their numbers are not limited by fluctuations in the availability of prey. Cats living completely without human contact or connection, however, may hunt only to feed themselves and their numbers are more affected by the availability of food sources.

Finding common ground among people holding such differing viewpoints can be a challenge.

In many parts of the country, as animal shelters have struggled to mediate such conflicts, they have seen the numbers of dogs and puppies in the community decline at the same time the numbers of cats and kittens either have not changed or have risen. This has prompted many shelters to reevaluate their programs dealing with cats and cats' impact on public health. In the past decade, the animal welfare movement also has engaged in a more vigorous debate about the euthanasia of healthy animals. In response, trap-neuter-return (TNR) programs have been adopted in some communities as one component of a comprehensive cat-care program.

The TNR approach, based on work in Denmark and the United Kingdom, sterilizes cats and then returns them to the location where they were trapped, as opposed to removing them for euthanasia or leaving them alone (Remfry 1996). The most structured form of TNR, in which levels of care are specified, is commonly referred to as Trap, Test, Vaccinate, Alter, Return, and Monitor (or Manage) (TTVAR-M). This level of care leads to what is referred to in this book as a *managed feral cat colony*. In the past several years, the AVMA (in the organization's policy statement approved in 1996)(AVMA 1997), the Cat Fanciers Association, the American Humane Association (in a 1999 policy statement), and The HSUS* have suggested that TTVAR-M is an alternative to the trapping and euthanasia of feral cats.

These issues—the impact of cats on wildlife populations, the efficacy and morality of euthanasia of healthy animals, the role that cats play in the community at large—all affect feral cat management. Although there are few things that everyone involved in the debate can agree on, there nearly always is some common ground.

1.2 Extent of the Problem

The size of the feral cat population is unknown. Differing interpretations of the terms "feral," "unowned," and "stray" make categorizing populations difficult, and geographic mobility complicates efforts to obtain an accurate count in any single community (Berkeley 2001). Two surveys on pet ownership undertaken in California provide estimates of the magnitude of the *unowned* cat problem. The 1993 study included a question about the number of unowned cats who were fed but not owned by the household. The responses indicated that 10 percent of households in Santa

Clara County fed cats that they did not own (Johnson et al. 1993). This included 49 households (47 percent) that did not own any cats. Survey respondents estimated that they fed 351 unowned cats, accounting for 40 percent of cats enumerated in the survey. The second survey, conducted in San Diego County in 1995, found comparable figures: 9 percent of households fed cats who they did not own, and these unowned cats comprised about 30 percent of all cats reported in the survey (Johnson and Lewellen 1995). In Massachusetts, over a three year period, 15 percent of pet-owning households fed cats who were not their own (Luke 1996). While some of these unowned cats may in fact be owned but free-roaming, they will nonetheless contribute to pet overpopulation and zoonotic disease transmission if they have not received veterinary care and are not sterilized and vaccinated.

Extrapolation to the entire U.S. population of stray and feral cats is not advisable, but these data do suggest that feral cat populations may be sizable in some parts of the country. Alley Cat Allies, one of the largest nonprofit feral cat advocacy organizations (see Resources), estimated that 30–60 million stray and feral cats live in the United States (Holton and Manzoor 1993).

Cat owners are exposed to issues surrounding feral cats via the media and the Internet. The range of publications for the general public includes information on specific programs and organizations (Allen 1998; Snapp and Glassner 1998; Viviani 1999), background on the issues (Tegner 1976; Donald 1992; Christensen 1997), and ways to help (Berkeley 1984; Berkeley 1990; Clifton 1992; Easterly 1998; Savesky 1999). Newspaper articles vary in their perspectives: a piece on established programs (such as Texas A&M University's Aggie Feral Cat Alliance of Texas, which appeared in the *Houston Chronicle* on October 11, 1998) or a statement on trapping and euthanizing cats (such as a *Daily Hampshire Gazette* story on a TNR program in South Hadley, Massachusetts, on October 10, 1998) are juxtaposed with debates on the pros and cons of TNR and the impact of cats on wildlife (such as *The Austin American Statesman* piece on May 4, 1997, and the Staunton, Virginia, *Sunday News Leader* piece on July 25, 1999).

A 2001 Internet search for "feral cats" revealed dozens of sites. Alley Cat Allies' Web site (*www.alleycat.org*) and that of the Feral Cat Coalition (*www.feralcat.com*) in California, for example, contained information and links to other key online sources.

Seminars on the local and national level have been organized by a range of agencies and organizations, including Alley Cat Allies and the San Francisco SPCA (SF SPCA), and jointly by the American Humane Association and the Cat Fanciers Association (Olson 1998). Alley Cat Allies was one of the first organizations on a national level to provide useful information on how to care for feral cats and to advise veterinarians working with such animals.

Feline-interest veterinarians are being drawn into the feral cat arena. At the Annual Feline Medicine Symposium held in 1999 at Texas A&M

University, practitioners were asked about feral cat care and management in their communities. Of the 63 who responded, 70 percent saw feral cats in their practices; 9.5 percent indicated that there was a formal TNR program in their locale (Dawn Fradkin, personal communication, May 19, 1999).

There is little data on the impact of feral cat predation on wildlife. One large wildlife hospital, however, reports that more than 20 percent of its 2,500 animals and birds are known to have been attacked by cats (Kaegel 1999). Wildlife rehabilitators report much lower percentages, but exact figures are impossible to determine since many owned cats may not bring prey home and unowned cats have unclear hunting patterns.

1.3 Sources of the Problem

Cats have become the most popular pet in the United States, with some 73 million cats owned (National Pet Owners Survey 2000–2001). Feral cats are part of a larger pet overpopulation problem that leads to the euthanasia of millions of unwanted cats each year. Feral cats both contribute to overpopulation and are victims of it—because cat owners view cats as an abundant, cheap commodity.

While sterilization rates in some parts of the country are high, many cats have litters prior to sterilization. One study in Massachusetts indicated that 91.5 percent of female cats were spayed and 90 percent of male cats were neutered, yet 15 percent of the sterilized females had had an average of two litters each prior to sterilization (Manning and Rowan 1998). Another Massachusetts study looked at why litters were born to owned cats (Luke 1996). The reasons, in order of frequency, were that the respondent could not afford to sterilize the cat, the respondent thought that the cat was too young to get pregnant, an indoor cat got out, the respondent didn't get around to sterilizing the cat, and the cat was still nursing kittens. A San Diego County (California) study reported that 84 percent of cats were sterilized; yet 19 percent of the females had a litter prior to being spayed (Johnson and Lewellen 1995). Fifty-eight percent of these litters were the result of owners not realizing that the cat was old enough to get pregnant or not realizing that the cat was in heat. Similar figures were reported in Santa Clara County (California) (Johnson et al. 1993). These figures indicate that cat owners must be educated about feline reproduction and that cats must be spayed or neutered as soon as possible.

Statistics on the numbers of cats who are acquired as strays or who leave the household by straying are another indication of the origins of feral cats. In a study in two western U.S. cities, 20 percent of cats left the household as strays (Nassar and Mosier 1986). In one of the same cities, seven of twenty-seven cats were acquired as strays (Nassar et al. 1984). In two studies in Massachusetts, 17 percent of cats were acquired as strays in 1991 and 17 percent of cats left the household by "disappearing" (Luke 1996).

A more recent study examined a national sample of 3,465 cat owning households (about one half of which were included because a pet had left the household the previous year). Among households that added a cat in the previous year, 21 percent of cats were acquired as strays, 19 percent as offspring of household's own cat and 14 percent from a friend (New et al. 2000). The same study found that among the 1,573 households where a cat had left in the previous year, 17 percent had had cats disappear, 13 percent had given a cat away, and 4 percent had relinquished the cat to a shelter or to animal control.

Some cats may be separated from their households—by being abandoned or being adopted into another home, for example—due to the range of personalities found among cats, even among those raised under similar circumstances. People may be initially attracted to a cat by his or her markings, colors, and coat rather than by his or her personality, only to find that an emotional bond with the animal never develops. One study of 47 cat owners evaluated their emotional attachment to a cat adopted from a shelter one year prior (Serpell 1996). This study found that less-attached owners felt that their cats were not affectionate enough. This was demonstrated by a large discrepancy between their "actual" and "ideal" ratings on a scale of affection compared to those of very attached owners.

The variation in personality, innate sociability, and effects of early socialization may explain the varied success rates in taming cats who have been born in, or spent time in, the wild. To cite one example, ten previously unsocialized cats of various backgrounds and ages now live in a house in Massachusetts. All of these cats were living in colonies, at least some of the cats were born to a feral mother, and all were socialized by the same person in the same house. Yet the cats in the household vary from those who are extremely well socialized, even with complete strangers, to those who only tolerate familiar people in the same room with them and hide if they see anyone else.

* The HSUS statement (Appendix B) is included as an example.

Definitions

Cats can, and often will, change their lifestyles during their lifetimes (Patronek 1998). A cat's lifestyle can be defined by four parameters: sociability spectrum, confinement status, ownership level, and location description. The first three parameters vary across a spectrum of behavior. They are designed to be functional in the context of the welfare and environment of the cats. Therefore, if all owned cats were kept indoors or confined to their owners' property, only unowned cats would remain free-roaming. But if more people were encouraged to become pet owners, more cats (who would now be owned) would be safely confined at home.

2.1 Sociability Spectrum

The sociability spectrum ranges from the two endpoints of (1) highly social (tame) pets, seeking attention from any and all people ("lap-cat" type) to (2) cats who have never had contact with people and are afraid of them (born in the wild, completely feral). Cats somewhere between these endpoints may also be afraid of people but have some interaction with them or may be at ease with some people but not seek attention. These estimations of sociability can also be related to where the cat is, since a veterinary office or shelter setting may make a cat who is well socialized in his or her home appear to be poorly socialized.

2.2 Confinement Status

Confinement status ranges from the two endpoints of (1) totally indoors to (2) always outdoors (Patronek 1998). Cats may be indoor/outdoor cats or spend some time outside but be confined to a pen, run, or fenced in yard during that time. (To reiterate, cats who are not confined to the house or an enclosure are *free-roaming*.) Feral cats are a subpopulation of free-roaming cats (Patronek 1998), unless they are confined to a sanctuary or sheltering facility.

2.3 Ownership Level

Ownership level ranges between the two endpoints of (1) a cherished pet cat with all the health care, food, and attention necessary, as well as a committed owner, to (2) cats who are completely unnoticed by any person (Miller 1996; Christiansen 1998). Cats existing between these two endpoints might include cats who have a person who claims ownership but does not provide more than the most basic care; cats who are cared for on a daily basis by a person but are free-roaming (for example, in a managed colony); "loosely-owned," "quasi-owned," or "marginally owned" cats who have been fed and cared for at some level but are not claimed by any person; and cats living in rural areas where they are valued solely for their rodent-control abilities. *Stray* cats (as defined in chapter 1.1) are free-roaming cats who are currently or recently owned but are lost or missing. Stray cats may be returned to their owners if the owners are looking for them or if they have some kind of identification. Stray cats not reunited with their owners may (1) be brought to a shelter or veterinary office to be adopted or euthanized; (2) be killed by cars, dogs, and other hazards; (3) be taken in by a new owner; or (4) remain free-roaming (and possibly become feral). *Abandoned* cats are strays whose owners deliberately leave them behind when they move or drop the cats at some other location. Stray cats usually are at least somewhat socialized following their initial separation from their owners. A *colony* of cats consists of three or more cats (not including young kittens).

2.4 Location Descriptions

Location descriptions include such colloquial terms as barn or farm cat, neighborhood cat, doorstep colony, or house cat. These terms have often been used to describe cats' level of sociability—a barn cat is a rural feral cat and an alley cat is an urban feral cat. But location descriptions are confusing, since, in some circumstances, the barn cat may be as well socialized, provided for, and loved as the indoors-only cat. It is proposed that these terms be restricted to location only.

Therefore, a house cat might be better described as an indoors-only, well-socialized, owned cat. A feral cat could be described as a free-roaming, poorly socialized cat who lives in a colony with a caretaker in a suburb. Any cat born "in the wild," unless caught and socialized (tamed), will start his or her life as a feral cat. Any free-roaming cat may become feral (less socialized) or contribute to the feral cat population if he or she is not sterilized. This means that any unsterilized owned, stray, or abandoned cat may increase the number of feral cats in the United States.

2.5 Sterilization Cost Terminology

The cost of sterilization has two components—what a cat caretaker or owner pays for the surgery and what it actually costs the clinic or veterinarian to perform the surgery. In programs where the owner or caretaker pays nothing or a low fee (less than $15), the surgery is often described as a *free* or *low-cost* spay/neuter. The actual cost of the surgery, however, is often more than the owner or caretaker pays. Someone else is paying the difference—the surgery is *subsidized*. In many private practices, the actual cost of materials and overhead for a spay is at least $30 (the veterinarian's time is often not included) and the fee charged ranges from $50–100 in urban areas to $30–60 in rural areas. In clinics that specialize in spaying and neutering, the volume of surgeries may allow the actual cost to be low enough so that a $30 spay (that is, $30 charged to the client) is not a subsidized procedure. In this situation, the surgery is truly *low-cost*.

Control or Management of Feral and Other Free-Roaming Cats

3

When feral or free-roaming cat populations are significant enough to generate complaints in a community, a local, state, or municipal agency will be tasked with responding. An agency's or organization's response will depend on the local ordinances; the resources available; the sophistication of the community regarding cats; the proportions of feral, socialized, and owned free-roaming cats; and the nature of the complaint. There traditionally have been four approaches to feral cats: (1) trap, remove, and euthanize; (2) trap, remove, and relocate to a new colony or place in a sanctuary; (3) trap, neuter, and return (TNR) feral cats to the original site (or the more complete management option, TTVAR-M); and (4) "wait and see." Socialized unowned cats may be placed in various settings for adoption or may be euthanized in any of these scenarios. Owned free-roaming cats can only be reunited with their owners if they have identification or if they are held in a shelter or otherwise made available for their owners to find them.

3.1 Trap, Remove, and Euthanize

Euthanasia of feral cats may be the only choice if the cats are sick or injured, are living in a place where they cannot stay or which is hazardous, or cannot be placed in ongoing care. In general, trap, remove, and euthanize is a short-term solution for any location unless the food and shelter that attracts the cats are removed from the habitat (Neville and Remfry 1984; Universities Federation for Animal Welfare 1995; Zaunbrecher and Smith 1993). If outside feeding by people, dumpsters, and other food sources is not eliminated, cats from nearby areas will move into the vacuum left by the cats who were trapped and euthanized (Tabor 1983; Passanisi and Macdonald 1990). Usually one or two cats elude the trappers and contribute to repopulating the area. This leads to repeated trapping and euthanasia cycles and does not provide a satisfactory solution. If, however, the habitat can be modified so that it is no longer attractive to cats—without easily available food sources or shelter—then removing the cats can be a long-term solution. Suggestions for habitat modification from the Peninsula Humane Society in San Mateo, California, include closing entrances to old buildings and holes under foundations; removing brush and junk that provide rodent hiding places; erecting fences; and repairing or blocking holes in windows and doors.

All cats and kittens should be removed from the buildings prior to sealing the buildings. The cats' movements can be determined by sprinkling flour near the exits and watching for tracks leading away from the exits. Although several commercially available repellents have been registered for use with cats, their efficacy is unclear.

3.2 Trap, Remove, and Relocate

Increasingly, agencies are turning to the second and third options, especially where previous trap and euthanize efforts have been unsuccessful or where public opinion is strongly against euthanasia.

Transfer to a new location is rarely recommended because finding a suitable site can be difficult, time consuming, and stressful for the cats and often has low survival rates at the new site. Sometimes, however, removal is the only alternative to euthanasia and some feral cat caretakers have successfully moved cats to new locations. Guidelines from Alley Cat Allies (2002a) state that transfer to a more rural, outdoor environment is viable if the cats cannot remain where they are. The organization describes six steps: (1) finding the new home; (2) trapping the cats; (3) providing veterinary care, including sterilization and vaccination; (4) transporting to the new location; (5) orienting cats to their new home; and (6) making follow-up contact. The orientation to the new location is imperative to get the cats to remain there. They should be confined in a building or enclosure for at least twenty-one days—until they consider that location to be their permanent feeding station. The Merrimack River Feline Rescue Society also has a very structured "barn placement" program for feral cats that must be relocated (see Resources).

Another sort of "transfer" is to socialize feral cats and place them in homes. This is possible to varying degrees with adult cats, but the time, patience, commitment, and number of appropriate homes needed are rarely available in sufficient quantities. Typically, previously feral adult cats will be socialized only with one or two people; however, on rare occasions, they may become well socialized with strangers. Kittens between eight and ten weeks of age are usually malleable enough to be tamed by a dedicated person. Alley Cat Allies (2002b), has produced an excellent fact sheet, "Taming Feral Kittens." Forgotten Felines of Sonoma County (see Resources) also provides guidelines for fostering and caring for feral kittens, as does the "Feral Friends" guide written by the president of the Rocky Mountain Alley Cat Alliance (formerly Denver Alley Cat Allies) and the SF SPCA's Feral Cat Assistance Program.

Sanctuaries are enclosed outdoor or indoor homes for long-term care of groups of cats. Sanctuaries may include cats who are partly or very socialized; a subset of these cats is often available for adoption to appropriate homes. In Hawaii, several dedicated cat caretakers have small sanctuaries on their properties where feral cats who could not be kept in their original location are housed in groups and receive care.

3.3 Trap, Neuter, and Return

The most basic form of TNR involves low-cost or subsidized sterilization for feral cats, as well as ear-tipping or notching and a rabies vaccination (when appropriate). No specifications are made for the level of follow-up care. In general, for TNR to be successful, three people are required: (1) a trapper to trap the cats, (2) a veterinarian to provide sterilization and vaccination, and (3) a caretaker to feed the colony and monitor it for new cats. Without monitoring, new cats will likely move into the colony and undo efforts to stabilize the population. Ear-tipping (or notching) permanently identifies the cat as sterilized. This practice will prevent any new caretaker from having to trap, transport, and pay for anesthesia or surgery for a sterilized cat and will protect the cat from the stress of being re-trapped and anesthetized.

For the full management program, TTVAR-M, all cats remaining in the colony should be (1) too unsocialized to place in a typical home; (2) tested for feline leukemia (FeLV) and feline immunodeficiency virus (FIV); (3) spayed or neutered (or be in the process of being trapped for that purpose); (4) vaccinated, at least for rabies; (5) provided with appropriate shelter, food, and water; and (6) monitored at least every other day by a concerned caretaker. Some guidelines also propose that the caretaker have the permission of the landowner to manage the colony at that location. In some cases obtaining consent is difficult, but it can provide legitimacy and protect the cats and the caretaker alike. There is some debate about the need for FeLV and FIV testing, particularly if funds are scarce and such testing will mean that fewer cats will be sterilized as a result. One opinion is that cats in an area should be tested for a period of time to establish the prevalence of FeLV and FIV. Another opinion is that rates of infection typically are low in feral cat populations and that spaying and neutering, since they will decrease fighting, will also decrease transmission of the diseases.

Philosophically, managed colonies should be considered an interim solution to the problem of feral, free-roaming cats—the first step toward reducing the size of the colony through attrition. In many cases, the initial step of removing tame adults and kittens will dramatically decrease the numbers of cats in the colony. Data from a 1992 Alley Cat Allies survey revealed that, of the 143 respondents who managed colonies using TNR, 60 percent of colonies stabilized or decreased in population (Holton and Robinson 1992). Where respondents indicated that populations had increased, the increases were attributed to the addition of lost, abandoned, or dumped cats and the difficulty encountered in trapping and spaying every cat in the colony. A colony will shrink only if all the cats are sterilized, so every effort should be made to capture every cat in the colony.

Managed colonies require a dedicated caretaker or caretakers. A caretaker should watch for health problems in colony cats (Passanisi and Macdonald 1990), trap and sterilize new feral cats, trap and remove new tame cats, and trap and remove kittens young enough to be socialized (usually those less than eight weeks old). While placing tame cats and kittens into good homes is the ideal, in some situations it can be surprisingly difficult, as can be finding suitable foster homes in which to tame the kittens.

Increasingly, the general public is becoming aware that there are alternatives to the euthanasia of feral cats and is supporting these alternatives. In some communities, support comes from organized groups that may be helpful in solving problems that arise. In other communities, negative publicity about trapping and euthanizing may trigger public outcry and lead to an alternative approach. Some animal welfare professionals, however, feel strongly that endorsing managed colonies legitimizes and makes acceptable the abandonment of unwanted cats. They are opposed to colonies under any circumstances. Both sides of this argument must be addressed by any community grappling with this problem.

3.4 "Wait and See"

Doing nothing—the "wait and see" or "let nature take its course" approach—historically has been the option that communities have used in dealing with feral cats, although often by default. In some cases, animal care and control agencies may have no mandate or ordinance to deal with feral cats. In other areas, no organized programs exist for managing feral cats, and the few caretakers who do exist are not coordinated in their efforts. Usually the "wait and see" approach results in continued breeding, increased cat mortality, continuing complaints by those near the colony, public health concerns, animal welfare concerns (often generated by high kitten mortality rates), and eventual financial costs in personnel, transportation, and euthanasia to animal care and control agencies and local governments.

Participants in Feral Cat Management

CHAPTER

Three groups play a role in managing feral cats: grass-roots advocates, service-providing and enforcement groups, and resource and education providers. These are not always clearly defined and mutually exclusive categories, but their functions must be filled in whatever management plan is adopted, whether it is trapping and euthanizing feral cats, transferring cats to a new location, or implementing TNR programs. Adopting "wait and see" as an official position, regardless of the reason for its adoption, typically leads to involvement of one or more of these groups, often made up of concerned or angry individuals who may decide to take matters into their own hands.

The role of veterinarians in control or management of feral cats can be crucial. While euthanasia of feral cats may not necessarily require a veterinarian, the sterilization of free-roaming cats does. Subsidized sterilization is required for managed feral cat colony programs to deal with the large numbers of cats. None of the other key groups can provide managed colonies without creating a link to local veterinarians.

4.1 Grass-roots Advocates

This group is made of individuals with an interest in feral cats, loose networks of caretakers, and established nonprofit organizations. These groups are usually focused on cat rescue and/or feral cat colony care, but other nonprofit animal protection organizations may be included. At the individual level, cat owners, shelter workers, volunteers, and veterinarians may all find themselves involved in various ways, including (1) caring for cats, (2) helping established groups, (3) developing policies about feral cats, or (4) starting nonprofit cat advocacy groups. In areas where there are a number of colony caretakers and people with an interest in feral cats, loose-knit networks may be formed. The members may alternate or trade feeding days, help each other with trapping, or cooperate in other areas of mutual interest and need. Until these networks become incorporated into recognized nonprofit 501(c)(3) groups, however, they will be limited in their ability to raise funds, gain public support, and interact with other community groups.

The established nonprofit organizations tend to have one of two philosophical approaches: providing a broad range of programs (trapping, sterilization, fostering, and adopting) or focusing on subsidized sterilization for a large number of feral cats. The first approach is illustrated by the SF SPCA's Feral Cat Assistance Program. The latter approach is exemplified by such groups as the Feral Cat Coalition in San Diego and Operation Catnip in North Carolina and Florida (see Resources). These programs offer free or low-cost subsidized sterilization once a month to anyone with a feral cat. Veterinary volunteers perform the surgeries, with 60–200 cats spayed or neutered, ear-tipped, and vaccinated in one day. The choice of approaches will vary with the organizers' interests and expertise, as well as with the availability of subsidized sterilization.

4.2 Service-Providing and Enforcement Groups

Animal shelters, veterinary clinics, animal industry businesses, and government offices are included here. For a community to be successful in dealing with feral cat problems, a spectrum of services must be available and affordable. No single type of intervention will have far-reaching effects.

Animal shelters—whether private, public, or private with a government contract—may be involved in managed feral cat colonies on many levels, from lending traps to providing trapping assistance or spay/neuter vouchers to coordinating feral colony management. They also may accept tame cats and foster feral kittens. Shelter programs may provide referrals to veterinarians or caretakers with expertise in feral cat work. They may hire veterinarians for in-house subsidized spay/neuter programs that can be used by feral cat caretakers. Cats can constitute more than half of all animals entering many shelters, and many shelters report that feral cats make up 20–50 percent of all cats entering the shelter, particularly those coming through animal care and control. Euthanizing feral cats, with or without a holding period, may constitute a significant percentage of cat-related euthanasias. Shelter personnel may work with other groups to modify or develop local ordinances. Shelter educational programs are crucial in preventing unsterilized, free-roaming cats and other sources of feral cats.

Veterinary clinics may provide spaying and neutering, perform euthanasias, and provide health care and advice to clients who deal with feral cats. There may be reduced-cost arrangements with established clients or groups, vouchers or coupons for subsidized spaying or neutering, or a commitment to low-cost surgical sterilization. Offering prepubertal spay/neuter is an important service to feral cat caretakers, since kittens over eight weeks old can rarely be tamed but should not be returned to the colony unsterilized. Studies on prepubertal gonadectomy demonstrate that sterilization of kittens as young as six weeks old is safe and practical (Aronsohn and Faggella 1993; Faggella and Aronsohn 1993). Rabies vaccinations, testing for feline leukemia and/or feline immunodeficiency virus, and advice on control of infectious diseases (especially respiratory) are also key services provided by veterinary clinics.

Animal industry businesses include providers of food, cages, microchips, traps and other handling equipment, and materials to build shelters for colonies. Pet food companies, home-and-garden retailers, and pharmaceutical companies may be willing to donate—or provide at reduced cost—products for feral cat caretakers, animal shelters, or veterinarians, especially if there is an incorporated cat care group or if approached by an appropriate shelter representative or veterinarian.

Government offices include public animal care and control agencies, public health agencies, state wildlife agencies, and any other office that may provide enforcement (such as police) or create ordinances that affect cats. The mission of animal care and control agencies is to protect the public from animal-related threats to health and safety and to protect animals from people. In some instances, this may be a difficult or nearly impossible mission, since cats may not be included under any ordinance or policy and may, therefore, be exempt from interventions by the animal care and control agency. In other jurisdictions, however, the agency may be in a position to provide a broad range of services, such as enforcement of local laws, humane trapping services, sheltering, public education, subsidized sterilization, registration of colonies, or assistance with managed colonies. Animal care and control agencies have the particular problem of having to convince the local government that funds them of the need for proactive approaches and the importance of investing money for long-term cost effectiveness, particularly when dealing with cats.

Public health agencies fit in many different places in various government structures, but they all have the same charge—to protect the health of the public. When talking about animals, this duty is most visibly carried out through rabies prevention, at least in most of the United States. Many other zoonotic diseases, however, are also of concern. Public health agencies may have laws about feeding or cleaning up after pets or about animals being present in certain locations. It is crucial to keep in mind that the individuals charged with protecting public health often view their jobs as preventive in nature. For example, because cats are known to be able to transmit toxoplasmosis in their feces, they believe that cats should not be allowed to defecate in public areas such as parks and beaches. Arguments about the low probability of transmission, the small percentage of cats that sheds the infective organism, or the low risk to most people for serious illness are not relevant or effective because toxoplasmosis *could* be transmitted to one person. That would be considered a failure to protect the public and could have legal ramifications. As a result, concerns about public health and free-roaming cats are unavoidable to some degree. (It must be remembered, however, that *all* free-roaming cats, not just feral cats, are potential disease transmitters.)

4.3 Resource and Education Groups

These individuals are often drawn from the previously mentioned groups. They are important for discovering and applying helpful, accurate, and timely information about all aspects of feral cat care and ecology. They may have years of experience in trapping feral cats or in starting grass-roots organizations or may have access to large networks of people with experience with feral cats. This group may also include scientists, some of whom are becoming involved in data collection and analysis on feral cat issues, or veterinarians specializing in feline care who contribute their knowledge of "herd health," public health, and general health care. Veterinarians can also play an important role by educating their clients on responsible pet ownership, including sterilization and safe confinement. Wildlife care and conservation organizations can provide information and public education about the health hazards and environmental impact of free-roaming cats through their education programs, which are often aimed at cat owners and wildlife enthusiasts. Sterilization and safe confinement are appropriate education themes for these groups, as well.

Community-Level Approaches

To address any feral cat problem effectively, fact-finding must take place and a multitude of services and programs must be enacted in the community (Christiansen 1998). Adding a single program, such as subsidized sterilization, is an excellent beginning but cannot be truly effective without educational programs, groups that foster cats and offer them for adoption, consistent involvement by colony caretakers, and cooperation among the various interest groups. Each community's approach must be tailored to its specific needs. Solutions often include some situation-specific legislative component; however, without services, education, and subsidies for those unable to afford to comply, the strictly legislative approach will not succeed. Such programs as TTVAR-M, voluntary identification through low-cost microchip clinics, a mobile spay/neuter van, or projects designed to help keep pets in their homes also can be developed for community-specific problem areas. In *Save Our Strays*, Christiansen (1998) includes nineteen programs that save animals' lives at the community and national level.

A brief examination of some community-level approaches illustrates how such programs can be tailored for communities at different stages of public awareness and acceptance and with different degrees of access to resources.

The Marin Humane Society (MHS) in Novato, California, has a variety of programs to serve animals adopted from the shelter and animals in the community. Each animal adopted from the shelter receives three weeks of free veterinary care provided by any of three local veterinarians familiar with shelter-related health problems. MHS also sterilizes and microchips all animals prior to adoption. For feral cats, free sterilization, microchipping, testing for FeLV and FIV (and euthanasia of positive cats), vaccinations, and tattooing (on the female incisions) are available from the shelter. Microchip clinics have been available since 1988 for community members with owned animals. Local veterinarians do not offer microchipping but will send clients to the shelter to get their pets microchipped. MHS maintains a database for returning lost pets to their owners.

MHS's other community programs include free sterilization for the pets of the disabled or elderly, low-cost subsidized sterilization, and monthly rotating cat sterilization clinics in the more remote parts of the county. MHS has an arrangement with many of the local veterinarians to perform a pre-determined number of subsidized sterilizations to handle any of MHS's overflow. An animal mediation service helps with cat-related complaints. One avid bird feeder, for example, had complained about his neighbor's cat coming into his yard. He was mollified once the mediator arranged for the neighbor to purchase fencing that kept the cat out.

These programs can be implemented in Marin County because of its residents' high level of education and income and their geographic distribution, and MHS has achieved impressive results. In 1980 MHS was handling 17,000 animals. In 1998 it handled about 5,000 animals and euthanized only 800 of them. The return-to-owner rate for cats in 1998 was 20 percent.

The city of Santa Rosa and the Humane Society of Sonoma County (California) designed and implemented a community-wide program to reduce the overpopulation of cats in 1992. This program included (1) a feral cat management pilot program; (2) a requirement that all animals adopted from the shelter be sterilized within thirty days; (3) shelter support for spaying and neutering at as early as eight weeks old; (4) ordinances requiring that outdoor cats be sterilized and prohibiting selling or giving away animals without a license; and (5) a voluntary identification program with collar and tags or microchips. An informational magazine was mailed to licensed pet owners and distributed at grocery stores and other places frequented by pet owners. Subsidized sterilization and pet food were made available for low- or limited-income pet owners. The shelter found that despite an increase in the city's human population, which usually leads to an increase in pets in the area and a resulting increase in shelter intake, the shelter's animal population began to decline. Two years after the program began, feline shelter intake numbers were down by 7 percent.

The SF SPCA is a well-known organization with a variety of programs that are made possible in part by a significant level of funding (about $10 per person in the city per annum) and in part by the staff's and board's willingness to try new programs and approaches. Its Feral Cat Assistance program has five main elements: (1) a subsidized spay/neuter program (with a $5 cash award), which includes testing for disease and vaccination; (2) workshops and a videotape series on trapping, cat advocacy, kitten care, socializing feral cats and kittens, relocation of feral cats, and medical issues (including a recently added twenty-four-hour voicemail information system); (3) cat assistance teams—networks of experienced people who can help novice caretakers; (4) free traps and food for cat assistance teams; and (5) cat advocacy (information on conflict resolution, protecting cats from complaints, etc.), which provides a help line, written material, and a $3,000 reward for information leading to the arrest and conviction of anyone abandoning a cat in San Francisco. The SF SPCA also has a limited-admission adoption center, free spay/neuter with $5 award for all cats in San Francisco, an animal behavior hotline, cat behavior videos and classes, a foster care program, a summer humane education "cat camp," free care for the pets of homeless residents, a pet-friendly housing program, and emergency preparedness classes for companion animal caregivers. The organization has sterilized more than 100,000 animals (including more than 8,000 feral cats) since the clinic began in 1976. The total euthanasia rate for the city (for both SF SPCA and the animal care and control facility) as of 1999 was 28 percent and is continuing to decline.

5.1 Legislation

The role of legislation in feral cat management in particular and pet overpopulation in general is controversial. Opinions on the issue range from "No law enforcement and regulatory approach will work" to "Legislation is the answer." Advocates of each position can point to successes and failures that support their conclusions. The effect of legislation depends on the community's opinions, resources, education level, and income, as well as other factors. In many locations, some sort of ordinance—such as requiring all cats from shelters to be sterilized before leaving the facility—is likely to be needed.

Even such seemingly straightforward and uncontroversial proposals as cat identification or mandatory sterilization of free-roaming cats can be complicated. What type of identification? For which cats? If for owned cats, what is the definition of "owned"? Who will pay for the personnel to enforce sterilization? How can one tell if a female cat has been spayed? Disagreement over such details can doom legislative initiatives before they are even written. Many ordinances are designed to be enforced primarily in response to a complaint rather than to be observed community-wide. Some enforcement agencies believe that this mechanism provides them with the opportunity to target problem areas and, particularly with "fix-it" tickets, resolve a specific problem when needed. Such ordinances give them the leverage to make a relatively small number of people do the right thing. Others believe that having ordinances that cannot be implemented or enforced community-wide undermines the legitimacy and efforts of their agencies. This is particularly true when large segments of the population are not in compliance and when limited funding and personnel are available for enforcement.

Some ordinances, such as "nuisance" ordinances, do not conflict with managed feral cat colonies. When carefully worded and implemented, they can be used to justify additional programs to provide assistance with feral cat problems and issues. Other ordinances, such as permits for custody or care of more than a certain number of animals (or "limit" laws), prohibitions against animals running at large, restrictions against "owned" animals in parks, and leash laws can make it impossible to gain the trust of and work with feral cat caretakers without special exceptions, since caretakers are likely to be in violation of these ordinances. If a community has an existing ordinance that forbids animals to run at large, then providing an exception to the feral cat caretakers creates a moral dilemma: how can it be acceptable for unsterilized feral cats to be running at large when an owner of a cat who is vaccinated and neutered will be penalized if the cat is found off the owner's property? There are arguments to be made both for and against an exception for feral cats from running-at-large ordinances, but both the original ordinance and the exception will certainly cause added conflict.

Legal Definitions of Ownership

Legal definitions of ownership—and even the use of this term rather than caregiver, guardian, harborer, caretaker, or similar alternatives—vary widely. In Connecticut and in Austin, Texas, if someone feeds cats on his or her property, even once, the cats belong to that individual. As owned animals, cats must to be licensed and vaccinated for rabies but do not need to have identification or wear the license tag. In Santa Rosa, California, an owner is someone who feeds and/or cares for an animal for fifteen consecutive days. In Charlotte, North Carolina, an owner is someone who is "keeping, having charge of, sheltering, feeding, harboring, or taking care of any animal for seven or more consecutive days" (City of Charlotte Animal Control Ordinance Sec. 3.3; 1/23/89). In Winston Salem, North Carolina, feeding an animal for seven days constitutes ownership. An ordinance in Palm Beach County, Florida (Animal Care and Control Ordinance 989–22), defines a "harborer or caregiver" as "any person or entity which performs acts of providing care, shelter, protection, restraint, refuge, food, or nourishment in such as manner as to control an animal's activities." Given the wide range of legal definitions—and in some locations, the lack thereof—it is not surprising that more personal definitions of ownership are also varied.

Feral Cat Registration

Registration of feral cat colonies or caretakers has been proposed and enacted in several locations with varied success. One animal shelter professional expressed support for registration because it meant that someone was caring for the cats and that the cats were vaccinated and neutered. But she pointed out that there might be complaints against the caretakers if the cats were in neighbors' yards killing birds or were bothering people near cat-feeding stations. She believed that part of the reason for having a monitored colony was so that the local animal care and control agency would know where the cats were and who was responsible for them; that way, if problems arose, they could be dealt with rationally. Registration does add some paperwork and creates the need for more definitions in a program. Caretakers have expressed varied opinions about registration, usually based on the level of trust and the quality of services provided in exchange for registration. Some feel that it is a win-win situation, while others are skeptical about the underlying motivation for or ultimate use of the registration information.

Palm Beach County, Florida; Cape May, New Jersey; and Santa Cruz and Novato, California, have cat registration ordinances of some kind. The Palm Beach County ordinance, passed in September 1998, was developed in response to a continuing increase in cats entering the shelter, about 20 percent of whom were feral. The ordinance requires owned, unsterilized cats to be confined to the owner's property; violators have the option of having the cat sterilized to waive the fine. Registered feral cat colonies, and caretakers in compliance with the feral cat component of the ordinance, are exempt. Requirements for registration include (1) annual renewal of each colony and payment of the fee ($10); (2) assurance that the cats are fed regularly year round; (3) sterilization of all cats and kittens between eight and sixteen weeks of age; (4) a good-faith attempt to remove kittens prior to eight weeks of age for domestication and placement; (5) removal of sick or injured cats for care or euthanasia; (6) ear-tipping all cats on the left ear and providing either a tattoo or microchip; (7) vaccination according to law (including rabies); and (8) proof of these medical requirements. As part of the ordinance, the department of animal care and control has the right to seize or remove the colony because (1) there are public health and safety concerns (including rabies); (2) the cats are creating a public nuisance; or (3) the feral cat caregiver fails to abide by the requirements. (The third component has caused a great deal of concern among the caretakers due their low level of trust in the department). Express permission of the property owner is not required.

Cape May, New Jersey, passed a feral cat protection ordinance with registration of caretakers in 1995. It allows people to care for feral cats if they register as caretakers, feed the cats regularly, trap and spay/neuter them, test them for FeLV and euthanize or remove those who test positive, ear tip them, and vaccinate them for rabies. There is no fee to register.

The director of animal control and code enforcement for the City of Cape May believes that the ordinance has reduced the number of feral cats and encouraged people to spay and neuter rather than just feed feral cats. It also has, in effect, given the director a specific charge to provide education and to work closely with feeders and caretakers to provide trapping, spaying and neutering services, and transportation to and from the veterinary clinic. Since no local veterinarian will provide subsidized spay/neuter services, the director takes cats to an Atlantic City clinic twice a month for such services. He has been able to provide half the cost of the surgeries through grants and other resources. This program, however, has only been successful because of the level of trust developed between caretakers and the agency.

The Novato, California, cat ordinance took effect in 1995 and includes a series of cat-related requirements. It defines a cat owner as any person who owns, keeps, or harbors an animal for fifteen or more consecutive days *(www.ordlink.com/codes/marinco/_data/title_8/04/020.html)*. All cats over four months old must be registered ($7 per cat to a maximum of $35). Microchipping is included with the registration; a collar and tag are optional. All outdoor cats over four months old must be sterilized. All violations are handled as "fix-it" tickets and are dismissed if the cat is registered and sterilized within twenty days (or longer if needed). Subsidized services are available to anyone who needs them. The feeling in this community is that the laws set a standard of care, and laws will pull noncompliers up to that standard. This type of law can establish "standing" for a particular cat who is in the care of someone and therefore not "vermin."

Even in the above locations, cat caretakers are a secretive group. They may have had cats—and themselves—threatened verbally and physically and they often feel isolated from the community. Because there is little public awareness of cat overpopulation or homelessness, one long-time caretaker and group organizer described caring for feral cats as "like a secret love affair." Caretakers may have a troubled history with animal control and other local officials, which makes them wary of any government involvement. In these situations, registration and other legal approaches are unlikely to have any positive effect and may actually serve to drive caretakers further underground. Without a major change in public opinion and government policy, the trust needed for this type of program will never develop.

Cat Licensing (Registration) versus Identification

Since dog registration (or licensing) has become well accepted (although not consistently enforced and effective), cat registration has been suggested as part of an effort to bring cats, feral or otherwise, under the same laws, with the same protections accorded dogs. Many ordinances do include provisions that require owners of unsterilized animals to pay a higher registration fee (commonly called differential licensing). Some require that all cats be vaccinated for rabies as a prerequisite for registration. Registration fees for sterilized cats typically range from no charge to $10, and for unsterilized cats from $10 to $50. Pet registration is generally perceived as something imposed on the owner by the government and lacking obvious benefits to the owner, so a cat registration ordinance can be extremely controversial until the benefits are well understood and accepted.

Identification programs, whether voluntary or mandatory, usually rely heavily on convincing pet owners that participation protects the safety and welfare of the pet. Ear-tipping of feral cats (left ear only or left for females and right for males), on the other hand, provides general identification of the cat as sterilized, and perhaps with a caretaker, but provides no unique identification of that cat. Microchipping is often suggested as a permanent, quick form of identification for any cat, but it is not visible—only shelters or veterinary clinics with scanners can tell if a cat has been chipped—and the cat can be traced back to the owner only if the chip is on file at a registry. The confidentiality of the information gathered and the viability of the various microchipping registries currently operating can also be problematic. New technology may address this latter concern by generating a chip that can lead directly back to the owner or caretaker without the registry acting as the middleman.

The traditional form of identification, collars and tags, do not work consistently on feral cats and are not recommended. Tattoos are sometimes used, but they fade over time and tattoo locations on the cat's body are not standardized. Ear tags and earrings have not yet been perfected.

Oahu, Hawaii, has a cat-identification ordinance that provides an owner with several ways to say, "This cat belongs to me." Microchip, collar and tag, and ear-notch or ear-tip are all acceptable, and identification provides the cat with a number of benefits should he or she end up in the shelter (a differential holding period, free ride home, etc.). The Hawaiian Humane Society invested time and effort to see what kind of approach would be acceptable to the community and the situation for the community's cats has been the better for it.

Beyond the logistical considerations of physical identification, crafting an ordinance acceptable to a particular community is important, especially where pet registration and identification issues are fraught with disagreement. Two adjacent towns in Massachusetts are a case in point. In one town, the residents were happy to pass an ordinance that required a registration fee as long as the cats did not have to wear tags. In the other town, residents did not want to pay a fee but did want the cats to wear collars and tags. Both approaches have strengths and weaknesses. The first option potentially generates revenue, but doesn't help reunite a lost cat with his or her owner. The second option creates paperwork without revenue, but outdoor cats with collars and tags can be returned to their owners.

Comprehensive Ordinances

Comprehensive ordinances are sometimes enacted at the city or county level but, because of their complexity, can only be effective if policymakers have done a great deal of planning and homework. A comprehensive ordinance is not a good approach for a community that is just beginning to grapple with cat issues, and it will only be successful if accurate information on the needs, opinions, and resources of the community is available.

The ordinance of San Mateo County, California, is one of the better-known examples. It (1) defines an "owner" as anyone who provides care or sustenance for thirty days or longer (except for barn or feral cat caretakers who are registered at no charge with the Peninsula Humane Society or San Mateo County Animal Control); (2) requires that all dogs and cats over four months old be vaccinated for rabies, licensed, and identified by a microchip, collar and tag, or other acceptable form; (3) requires that all dogs and cats over six months old be spayed or neutered unless the owner has a license for an unaltered animal or a license and permit for breeding; and (4) requires that any person offering dogs or cats for sale or adoption have the proper licensing, registration, and permit information (among other specifications and restrictions), except for rescue and adoption agencies. Total intake of cats at the Peninsula Humane Society, the main shelter serving San Mateo County, has been gradually decreasing, to one-third fewer cats in 1999 than in 1991, and return-to-owner rates for cats gradually increasing, from 3 percent in 1991 to 4.5 percent in 1998. The number of cats euthanized also decreased by 10 percent in this period.

Sterilization

Sterilization of all animals adopted from animal shelters has become standard in recent years. At least twenty-one states have made it a requirement, and many shelters in other states sterilize all their animals as part of their programs. Some shelters sterilize all animals before leaving the shelter, while others send animals home intact but require their new guardians, via a signed contract, to have the adopted animals sterilized. Compliance rates for owner sterilization vary; 50 percent is a commonly cited figure. Even a 90 percent compliance rate means, however, that 10 of 100 animals could have a litter before being spayed or neutered. Even if only two litters are born from every 100 adopted animals, this can quickly add up. Shelter personnel are then contributing to the very problem that they are trying to solve. It is crucial for all shelters to make a serious effort to get all animals sterilized before they leave the facility.

Some states have also instituted incentive laws for spaying and neutering. A portion of the funds collected from pet registration fees or special "I'm animal friendly" license plates goes toward subsidized programs.

Mandatory sterilization of all cats (and dogs) over a specified age, or of all free-roaming or outdoor cats, is another approach. El Dorado, Arkansas; Montgomery County, Maryland; Petaluma, California; Bloomington, Indiana;

and Oneonta, New York, have ordinances requiring that free-roaming cats be sterilized. Fines vary, with some set at several hundred dollars and others with explicit "fix-it" components, which waive penalties if the owner takes action to comply with the ordinance. Camden, New Jersey; Denver, Colorado; and King County, Washington, require dogs and cats over six months old to be sterilized. Typically, permits are available for exceptions to these sterilization ordinances. Violators in Camden may be subjected to fines as high as $1,000 and/or imprisonment of up to ninety days and/or up to ninety days of community service. King County offers a $25 spay/neuter voucher with each unaltered license. Washington State tracks animal shelter statistics, and it has found not only that the total numbers of animals entering shelters remained steady between 1992 and 1997 but also that adoption and return-to-owner rates were rising and euthanasia rates dropping.

Local, regional, and state government can be involved in feral cat issues in a wide variety of ways. In most cases, the government is reacting to pressures or problems presented by groups in the area. In other situations, the government is taking the lead in developing more sophisticated approaches for cat problems in the area. Again, knowledge of the local situation is crucial for well-received, effective approaches.

6
CHAPTER

Issues Surrounding Feral/Free-Roaming Cats

6.1. Public Health Concerns

Any free-roaming cat can potentially spread zoonotic diseases (Olsen 1999). Public health agencies are charged with protecting the public against all diseases that can be transmitted between animals and people. The problems most commonly encountered in the context of feral cats are bites—particularly given concerns about rabies, toxoplasmosis, plague, toxocariasis, ringworm, and bartonellosis. (It is important to remember that feral cats are only part of the free-roaming cat population and that confining owned animals and protecting them from, or treating them for, these zoonoses is also necessary to ensure public health.)

Cat bites can be painful and usually become badly infected if they are not treated appropriately. Truly feral cats will only bite people if they have been cornered or trapped and caged. Most bites are suffered by inexperienced caretakers or members of the general public who try to pat or pick up an animal or corner an animal while trying to pat or catch him or her. Common sense and education will prevent most cat bites among the general public, caretakers, shelter personnel, veterinary employees, and others who work with cats.

In most parts of the United States, rabies is by far the most serious consequence of a cat bite. It is a disease that almost any warm-blooded animal can contract, but because of certain disease characteristics and vaccination patterns, it is more common in some species than in others. With the advent of effective vaccines for domestic species and better prevention and treatment in people, the risk of contracting rabies from dogs has decreased. An increasing number of cats, however, have been diagnosed with rabies in the past several years—more than twice as many cats (300) as dogs in 1997 (Krebs et al. 1998). Among the twenty-two large-scale human exposures to rabid or potentially rabid animals between 1990 and 1996, three were the result of interaction with cats (Rotz et al. 1998). Most of these large-scale exposures could have been avoided if very young animals with unknown medical histories or those who had only recently been vaccinated had not been taken to public facilities and handled by many people. Such large-scale exposure to feral cats is only likely to occur if young kittens being fostered or offered for adoption are taken to schools or parties while they are incubating the disease. Nearly 93 percent of reported rabies cases in 1997 were in wild animals and none of the rabies cases in people between 1990 and 1997 was caused by cats (Krebs et al. 1998).

Feral cats are vulnerable to intervention by public health agencies because of the serious ramifications of rabies. Inexperienced feral cat caretakers and the general public should be cautioned against cornering or trying to handle unknown free-roaming cats. Caretakers and other individuals working with feral cats should consider a pre-exposure vaccination against rabies; however, the cost and availability of vaccines make this problematic except for individuals whose professional work involves handling potentially unvaccinated cats. Cats in managed colonies (except in Hawaii and countries where rabies is not found) should be vaccinated for rabies at the time of sterilization, using a three-year vaccine. Caretakers should make serious efforts to recapture cats in their colonies to revaccinate at three-year intervals. Because many cats become more social with their caretakers over time, revaccination should be possible for the majority of cats. By keeping a critical mass (usually 80 percent) of feral cats vaccinated against rabies in managed colonies, a herd immunity effect may be produced (Hugh-Jones et al. 1995), potentially providing a barrier between wildlife and humans and preventing one of the major public health threats caused by feral cats.

Toxoplasmosis, an increasing concern, is also not specific to feral cats (Patronek 1998). The estimated prevalence of *Toxoplasma gondii* antibodies in cat blood is variable, likely due to the different populations tested and the choice of tests. The prevalence of antibodies in the blood of various groups of free-roaming cats have been reported at 11 percent, 33 percent, 68 percent, and 80 percent (Dubey and Weigel 1996; D'Amore et al. 1997; Hill et al. 1998; Nogami et al. 1998). A study conducted in Norway indicated that living in a neighborhood with cats is not by itself a risk factor for contracting toxoplasmosis (Kapperud et al. 1996). (The oocysts shed in the cat feces are the only stage of the toxoplasmosis organism that is infective to humans.) While vaccines to prevent the shedding of oocysts in cats are being studied, no real prevention is currently available (Olsen 1999; Dubey 1996). Because most cats only shed oocysts for a few weeks after primary (that is, their initial) infection, young cats who hunt are most likely to be spreading the disease (Dubey and Weigel 1996; Dubey 1996). It is possible that keeping feral cats in well-managed colonies where food is provided and no kittens are born could decrease the shedding of oocysts into the environment by these cats.

Plague *(Yersinia pestis)* is a disease that is also on the rise, although it is geographically limited. Humans most often contract the disease through contact with infected fleas, but contact with infected animals—including cats—may also result in infection (Cleri et al. 1997; Lopez 1997). Feral cats in the southwestern United States, because they are likely to hunt and to be in proximity to rodents and fleas, can be at risk for plague (Patronek 1998). Flea control in feral cats in these parts of the United States may be a wise precaution. Care in handling feral cats who appear to have pneumonia will decrease the risk contracting the disease (Eidson et al. 1991).

Toxocariasis, a disease caused by abnormal migration of roundworm larvae in people, is also not confined to feral cats. Owned cats may have roundworms, and dogs can contribute to the problem. While recommendations have been made that dogs and cats with roundworms not be allowed to roam, enforcement is difficult, so this disease has not been controlled (Hendrix et al. 1996; Schantz 1994).

Ringworm is most likely to be a problem for caretakers who are treating injured or ill feral cats or fostering kittens. It is a self-limiting disease, with most cats self-curing within six months. For most humans, ringworm is not a serious health problem.

The *Bartonella* bacteria can produce a variety of clinical diseases in people, the most recognized of which is cat-scratch disease (Breitschwerdt and Kordick 1995). The risk level of contracting bartonellosis from cats remains unclear. Because free-roaming kittens have been implicated in the spread of the disease, however, those who foster kittens may be at highest risk (Patronek 1998; Breitschwerdt and Kordick 1995).

6.2 Impact on Birds and Wildlife

Free-roaming cats are often portrayed as hunting machines and are frequently mentioned as possible causes of declining bird populations and biodiversity. It is not clear from existing data on non-island ecosystems whether cats have an impact on wildlife at the species level. Many free-roaming cats do kill individual birds, mammals, reptiles, and amphibians. It is unknown whether cats in managed colonies change their hunting patterns after being sterilized. The literature does suggest that cats are opportunistic feeders and will eat whatever is handy and plentiful, including garbage, cat food, and carrion (McMurry and Sperry 1940; Laundre 1977; Mitchell and Beck 1992; Mirmovitch 1995; Fitzgerald and Turner 2000).

Because some cats (feral or otherwise) are fed by people, they are not regulated by the availability of food in the ecosystem in the same way that wild predators are. The hunting patterns of cats in each type of ecosystem and the effects of sterilizing feral cats in managed colonies on these patterns is unknown. The impact of cats on wildlife in urban environments will also be quite distinct from other settings, because most birds and animals found in inner cities are considered pests or are themselves non-native species.

Studies of cats and prey fall into three categories: those of island ecosystems, those of free-roaming owned cats, and those of mostly feral cats. These studies have been conducted in a variety of habitats and have used many different study designs; as a result, the authors themselves often caution against extrapolation or point out sources of bias (Mead 1982; Dunn and Tessaglia 1994; Patronek 1998). Yet the results are often extrapolated (Coleman and Temple 1989; Mitchell and Beck 1992) and sensationalized (Harrison 1992). The accuracy and application of these studies depends on the location (farm, suburb, wilderness area, or city), the number of cats studied (6 versus 100), the type of cats (owned indoors-outdoors, feral, fed, somewhat socialized barn cats, etc.), and the study method. These studies cannot be used to make sweeping statements about the numbers of prey killed or the impact of cats on wildlife in situations that are not similar.

In mainland ecosystems, no published data have shown that cats have a detrimental impact on wildlife populations of particular species. In many cases, the cats are one of many predators (Fitzgerald 1988) and may be filling the role of some other small predator that is no longer present (Coman and Brunner 1972; Mead 1982). In fact, habitat destruction is cited as the most serious problem for birds (Terborgh 1992; Robinson 1998). Pollution, competition from other bird species, and predators such as raccoons and opossums are other major challenges (Terborgh 1992). Window collisions and hunting of birds by cats are much lower on the list of causes of bird deaths (Robinson 1998). Cats do kill some birds and could contribute to a limited degree to population declines. Nonetheless, conclusions about the impact of cats on wildlife and birds at the species level can only be made when enough location-specific data have been collected and analyzed.

In some sensitive habitats, cats (feral and otherwise) may be a threat to specific species, particularly ground-nesting birds. But cats are only one piece of a complex system. As a parallel example, a biological assessment undertaken in the late 1990s indicated that non-native red foxes were one of several predators and many other dangers to a particular bird species. Yet the proposed solution was to establish a five-year predator-control program aimed at the foxes, which, it turns out, had never been seen living in that particular location. This type of single-minded approach creates unnecessary hostility and does not address the underlying problems. To protect habitats, people must address all the causes of destruction and predation.

Hawaii is the only state in the United States that must deal with the impact of feral cats on island ecosystems. The islands are home to thirty species of endangered birds and three species (rats, feral pigs, and the deliberately introduced mongoose) that are considered to be predators serious enough to cause problems in sea and forest habitats. Cats are likely only a problem during a limited crucial period for ground-nesting birds and are unlikely to be a threat to birds that nest high up.

On one level, the debate about cats and wildlife becomes a question of philosophy and morality. Allowing owned cats to hunt clearly reflects the owners' belief that their cats' need or right to hunt takes precedence over the protection of vulnerable wildlife species. In theory, owned cats could relatively easily be prevented from killing wildlife by being confined to the house or an enclosure or by going out only on leash. Preventing unowned cats or those who are too unsocialized to be kept in a house from hunting is more difficult. Trap and euthanize as a strategy has the drawbacks outlined previously.

Education will be central to any solution to the problem of cats and wildlife predation, but changing people's opinions and ideas is a slower process. The issues are often couched in emotional terms: My cat is unhappy inside; he needs to hunt; I don't want to clean a litter pan; my cats have always gone outside. Such beliefs are usually not easily altered by rational arguments and facts.

6.3 Welfare of the Cats

The risks that feral cats face depend on the environment in which they live. Such hazards as cars, dogs, people, wild predators (particularly coyotes in some parts of the country), and diseases are real and can kill or injure free-roaming cats. In some cases, feral cats are wild enough to decrease the likelihood that they will be caught by abusive people or hungry predators, but not always. Keeping owned cats indoors, confined to a pen or yard, or on a leash will likely extend their life span considerably. Although most socialized cats will be healthy and content in an appropriate habitat, an indoor or confined lifestyle is rarely an option for feral cats and may not be suited to their disposition.

Several techniques can help to protect free-roaming cats from wild predators. These include keeping feeding areas clean and limiting the time and amount of food available to avoid attracting other animals, installing "cat posts" (sturdy climbable wooden posts six to eight feet tall), or erecting fencing to exclude predators from the area (Hadidian et al. 1997).

Beyond the issue of safety, concerns about quality of life often arise in discussions about feral cats. There are three conflicting schools of thought. One is that the cat is a domestic species and thus must have ongoing contact with a caretaker or owner to be happy. Another is that cats easily revert to the wild and adapt to a variety of conditions; they are free spirits and to cage or confine them is cruel. The third is that cats living on the street lead miserable, unsafe lives and the most humane solution is to trap and euthanize them.

Such debates occur because a definition of quality of life has yet to be developed. Another reason is the basic assumption that life—sometimes regardless of the "quality"—is better than death, even by euthanasia. Without scientific data, resolution of these arguments can only be based on emotion and personal experience. In some circumstances, however, obvious indicators of health—such as body weight; coat condition; the presence or absence of discharge from the eyes, nose, ears, and mouth; and FeLV and FIV status—do suggest whether specific cats are doing well or poorly and can be used to support decisions made for those particular cats.

Socializing or confining adult feral cats can have mixed results. Some feral cats can become tame enough to live in homes, even becoming so well-socialized that a stranger would have no idea that the cat used to be feral. Such occurrences are relatively rare, however, because most people do not have the expertise and patience to socialize a feral cat. Most feral cats remain poorly socialized, regardless of the owner. Some feral cats are permanently housed in sanctuaries. Properly designed and maintained, these sanctuaries can provide a high quality of care for the cats, and most seem to adapt. Not everyone, however, has the knowledge, facilities, time, and money to provide a high level of care and to prevent overcrowding and contagious disease problems. These sanctuaries are quickly filled. Moreover, poorly run and designed sanctuaries raise questions about the quality of life on those premises.

Vaccination will reduce the probability of disease transmission from feral cats to socialized owned cats or wild felines. One report of a cougar with FeLV in California and another on seropositivity of Florida panthers for panleukopenia and FIV have been published (Patronek 1998). No definitive sources for the viruses were determined and other wild carnivores may have been involved rather than domestic cats.

6.4 Management of Existing Colonies

Whether a cat leads a good life in a managed colony is a continuing debate, partially because data on life expectancy and disease frequency are lacking. It seems clear that in the right location and with a dedicated caretaker, feral cats in managed colonies can lead a good life—that is, as good or better than some owned cats. Some colonies have cats born into them who live a decade or more. Many are in good health, are of optimal weight (or even overweight), have bright eyes, and move normally. They may have become tame to their regular caretakers, allowing themselves to be petted and sometimes even picked up. The cats know the feeding routine, the call of their caretaker, or the sound of their caretaker's car, and wait, sometimes impatiently, for their meals. Some caretakers provide flea and tick control for cats who are particularly sensitive to parasites or ongoing control for internal parasites such as roundworms and hookworms. A few feral cats will let a quiet stranger approach if their caretaker is present, especially if the cats have been in the colony for some time.

In a 1992 survey by Alley Cat Allies, more than 90 percent of the responding caretakers said that the health of the feral cats that they encountered was good or excellent (Holton and Robinson 1992).

A well-managed colony in a community can lead to abandonment of cats by owners who believe that their cats will be cared for in the colony. Although many locales have ordinances prohibiting abandonment, the ordinances are notoriously hard to enforce. Prominently posted signs at high-visibility locations may deter a subset of cat owners from leaving their animals. In some locales, cat-only or limited-admission shelters may provide a more acceptable place to relinquish cats than an open-admission shelter. Programs to provide assistance with placing cats in new homes may also deter "dumping." Many caretakers try to keep their colony's existence secret or at least decrease its visibility by feeding in sheltered areas, concealing cats' sleeping shelters, and feeding at night. Unfortunately, cats will be abandoned whether or not managed colonies exist if the owner (1) is not attached to the cat; (2) does not feel that there are alternative homes available or is unable or unwilling to search for homes (by placing classified ads in local newspapers, for example); (3) has a poor understanding of animal shelters and their availability or services; or (4) lacks knowledge of the dangers to free-roaming cats. Most managed colonies need to have some mechanism in place to deal with tame adult cats who suddenly appear in the colony, either because they were abandoned or because they strayed too far from home with no identification.

It is crucial that the colonies be well managed (based on the preceding guidelines) for the optimal health and safety of the cats and the environment. Individuals who feed cats but do not get them neutered and do not visit them on a regular basis are doing more harm than good, and, in fact, contribute to the feral cat problem. In some circumstances, feeding facilitates increased breeding and the resulting kittens often have a high mortality rate. Some colonies in the early stages of trapping and sterilizing have very high rates of diseases—particularly upper respiratory disease—with more than 50 percent mortality in kittens under one year old. Established, managed colonies do not have any kittens born into the group (although some may migrate in or be abandoned in the area) and the general health of colony cats is often good.

In Santa Rosa, California, Forgotten Felines of Sonoma County has helped manage feral cats in a number of parks. In one park with more than fifty cats, good management reduced the number to eight cats for three consecutive years. In another park, trapping and euthanizing about fifty cats every one to two years kept the population steady at one hundred or so cats. Since no animals were supposed to be living in the park, however, this situation was still unacceptable. Caretakers and park officials worked together to address the problem, jointly choosing the location and type of feeding stations and shelters to be offered. Caretakers removed food and water at night to discourage wild animals from scavenging. Two years after the local feral cat group began working with the director of parks, the population had stabilized at eleven, and no kittens had been born.

Unless caretakers intend to find indoors-only homes for feral cats, keeping the cats fairly timid around people, particularly strangers, is a good idea for the cats' own safety. Although some tame cats may live in safe colony locations and are as well cared for as any owned indoors/outdoors cat, others live in hazardous areas. In such areas, there often are not enough decent homes, and no organizations exist to help place cats in homes. The dilemma for caretakers in such circumstances is whether to keep the cats in the colony where the caretakers see, feed, and play with the cats every day; euthanize healthy cats; or place the cats into less than ideal homes, in which they would possibly receive a lower standard of care than in the colony. This dilemma is more common than one might expect—and heartbreaking to resolve.

The TTVAR-M approach for feral cats can improve their health and their interactions with people in many situations. When stringently carried out, this approach should help prevent future generations of cats from being in the same situation. Sterilizing cats reduces yowling, fighting, and spraying, and sterilized cats spend less time and energy looking for mates, having kittens, and competing for territory (Kristensen 1980; Remfry 1980; Royal Holloway College University of London 1981; Zaunbrecher and Smith 1993).

6.5 Human Perceptions and Needs

Cats' relationships with people range from being treated as child surrogates to being condemned as vermin. Cats are viewed as companions, friends, charming rural inhabitants, working animals to control pests, and pests themselves. These relationships color people's views on how cats should be cared for. A panel of experts sponsored by The HSUS came to a consensus on a core belief: that cats are domestic animals, not wildlife, and require care and control for their safety and for the protection of wildlife. The increasingly large number of cats kept as indoors-only pets supports a slowly-spreading acceptance of this view in the United States. While many cats can adapt to be free-roaming, wild animals by filling niches in the ecosystem, particularly in more rural settings, this should not be viewed as a long-term role for cats.

Farm and stable owners likely will always maintain small groups of free-roaming cats for rodent control. Cats in such circumstances may be highly valued for their working ability and may have been purposefully acquired for the location. They may also be living exclusively or primarily on the owner's property, which decreases the likelihood of problems with neighbors. The minimum level of care for these cats, however, should include feeding, vaccination, spay/neuter, treatment of injuries, social interactions, and protection from the elements. Such cats, in most areas, will have a limited impact on wildlife other than on "pest" species, and feeding and socialization would encourage them to stay close to their home.

A well-documented example of this situation is Pennsylvania's Longwood Gardens, where cats are part of the integrated pest management control program to protect certain plant life from damage by small rodents. The cats were originally strays. They now have a home range, a building for shelter, and a caretaker. If one accepts the premise that rodents need to be controlled for the sake of the gardens, then these cats have done an excellent job. The cats' rodent-control success has been rewarded with the value placed on their continuing presence, the play times they enjoy, and the high standard of medical care provided for them.

6.6 "Nuisance" Issues

Nuisance complaints about free-roaming cats are common for animal care and control agencies and, at times, for local governments. Complaints include such behaviors as spraying, fouling yards and gardens with feces, yowling and fighting; sick, injured, or dead cats; and dirty footprints on cars. Some of these problems decrease when cats are sterilized, but others will occur wherever free-roaming cats are found. Some people hate cats and will be unhappy whenever any cat is outside. Others can be engaged in mediation, which can achieve the goals of both the complainant and the caretaker or owner. (The SF SPCA offers suggestions for resolving problems informally in a fact sheet, "Neighbor Conflicts.")

Managed colonies of feral cats can be part of the solution to nuisance complaints. One animal control agency in Florida found that cat complaints in a six-square block area were cut in half the year after a TTVAR-M program was instituted (personal communication, Linda Haller, February 24, 1999). In the city of Cape May, New Jersey, complaints about cats dropped by more than 50 percent in the four years since well-managed feral cat colonies were established by the feral cat protection ordinance (personal communication, John Queenan, June 6, 1999). According to the Feral Cat Coalition in San Diego, between 1992 (when the program began) and 1997, the number of cats impounded and euthanized by the San Diego Department of Animal Control decreased by almost half. Before a high volume spay/neuter program began, these euthanasia statistics had been rising by 15 percent each year. In Sonoma County, California, a requirement to sterilize outdoor cats, combined with the managed feral cat program, reduced the number of cats coming into the shelter by 7–11 percent. In Louisiana, one local district animal control agency that had many nuisance complaints about cats saw calls drop by 80 percent after eight months of intensive community involvement, trapping of feral cats, and subsidized spay/neuter clinics (including a mobile unit). After ten months, nuisance calls had all but stopped.

Grass-roots Approaches

7.1 Levels of Involvement

Grass-roots involvement can be defined as any activity or interest on the part of private citizens, as opposed to programs that are legislated or implemented by an interest group. Grass-roots cat organizations are groups with a strong focus on cat rescue and feral cat care. General animal welfare organizations without a physical facility may fall under this definition if they work with cats. People can be involved at the grass-roots level as individuals, as loosely knit networks with shared interests, or as incorporated Section 501(c)(3) (under the IRS code) nonprofit groups. As individuals (cat owners, feral cat caretakers, shelter workers or volunteers, veterinarians, etc.), people can work individually on their interests or link with other people to accomplish larger goals. They also can be involved at a very personal level with their own animals by providing identification, vaccinations, and sterilization; taking responsibility for a pet's actions; and providing the animal with life-long care (Christiansen 1998).

Many individuals start working with feral cats and feral cat groups accidentally. They may find themselves feeding a few cats at work or in their neighborhood, or they may notice neglected cats in a park or industrial area. Some people realize right away that they must find ways to spay and neuter these cats, while others only begin to look at the larger picture beyond feeding the cats after seeing kittens die or meeting with caretakers who are familiar with TTVAR-M programs. Most individual involvement expands into involvement with established programs of some kind, reading and learning more about feral cats, caring for cats in various settings, or starting new groups.

In many parts of the country, having cats spayed and neutered is neither easy nor inexpensive. Encountering these barriers may lead individuals to develop subsidized spay/neuter programs, to organize others to provide needed services, or to educate the community about the problems of feral cats. While loose-knit groups have the advantage of being able to share knowledge, ideas, expertise, and connections, these groups can have only limited impact in terms of legitimacy and focus if they are not incorporated.

The lack of an organization, however, needn't prevent action. All that is needed to begin to stabilize the number of feral cats in a colony is a willing veterinarian (to perform spays/neuters, vaccinations, and ear-tipping/notching), someone to trap the cats and transport them to the veterinarian, and a caretaker to feed the cats—preferably on a daily basis—and watch for new intact cats who will need to be trapped and sterilized. Feeding the cats regularly will keep them from roaming as much, improve their bond with the caretaker, and facilitate monitoring of the colony. Without some kind of monitoring, new, unsterilized cats who are abandoned or stray will increase the number of cats and kittens in the colony.

Established 501(c)(3) nonprofit organizations can have a larger impact in a community than an individual if there are members with good organizational and interpersonal skills. These groups will usually find it easier to network with other community organizations, such as shelters and local veterinary associations, and may have more influence with local government. They also are likely to be more effective at large-scale fundraising. Funding sources include membership fees, donations, mailings, bake sales, thrift shops, and special events.

Effective community-wide feral cat programs must be multifaceted. They must include subsidized spay/neuter programs, shelters for owned cats, options for adoption and fostering partially socialized cats and kittens, information for feral cat caretakers, good relationships with existing animal protection groups, and support from veterinarians. If adoption is part of the group's mission, it needs to think carefully about its adoption policies. Will the group take the cat back under any circumstances? Will the group permit adoptions into homes that will allow the cat outdoors or declaw the cat? Will the group allow a home with three or more cats to adopt? Local programs and humane societies may already have good adoption guidelines available to adapt to the program. National humane organizations can also provide advice, as can local programs such as the Rocky Mountain Alley Cat Alliance. Some communities have ordinances about the transfer of ownership; it may be necessary for the previous owner of an animal to give permission or for the animal to be processed and held for the proscribed period of time (to allow an owner to claim the animal) by the local humane society or animal care and control agency. Recognized nonprofit organizations may be able to satisfy the holding period requirement (which allows an owner to claim the cat) without bringing the cat into a shelter.

7.2 Developing Groups

The Neponset Valley (Massachusetts) Humane Society publishes an excellent guide—*How to Create a Grass-roots Community Program to Help Feral Cats* (see Resources). Authors Bonney Brown and June Mirlocca observe that organizations, rather than individuals, tend to attract attention and donations, can be easily mobilized in the face of a threat, and can provide emotional and informational support to solitary caretakers. Working locally on a problem, the authors believe, has a greater impact and allows residents to see causes, effects, and solutions. The authors' detailed, step-by-step information on starting a program is recommended reading for anyone thinking about creating a local group. Operation Catnip's *Guidebook and Policy Manual* also has useful information on educating communities on TTVAR-M programs, starting spay/neuter groups, and formulating budgets (see Resources).

All grass-roots feral cat organizations originate because someone is concerned about cats, either generally or as the result of some personal interaction. One dedicated person with good interpersonal skills can get other people together, and then a well-organized person can get interested members to stay on track and find common ground. Once a mission has been set, the group must stay focused: it is easy to spread too thin trying to be all things to everyone. To avoid this pitfall, the group should maintain lists of other organizations and agencies that can provide the services that the group cannot. Recorded phone messages should clearly state what the group is and isn't able to do. Express the group's focus in a clear, written format, including, if appropriate, the number of cats involved in the group's efforts. A working relationship with at least one veterinarian is a necessity, since feral cat care requires veterinary expertise—and a veterinarian can be a powerful ally.

There will be both immediate local concerns—for example, the care of one particular cat or colony—and larger community or regional concerns—for example, the need for community-wide education. It is easy to get bogged down in the daily needs of the animals and not recognize the larger context of the problem.

There will always be some opposition to feral cat programs. Once the program succeeds, much of that opposition will dissipate. Sometimes, a neutral party can identify common ground; at other times, bringing as many interests on board as possible can be useful. In some situations, starting quietly and showing what the program can do is the best approach. Large-scale programs often benefit from having someone involved who is already trusted by the cat caretakers in the area. This gives the program an advantage in connecting with feral cat caretakers.

A skilled writer can draft the working guidelines for the organization and write materials for distribution outside the group. If this person has a vested interest in the issue or is respected for his or her work or background, even better. One of the founders of a Massachusetts program that began in 1982 on the grounds of a school believes that it succeeded in getting the school administration on board and the regional SPCA to provide start-up assistance because the main contact person was a long-time employee of the school. One program in California may have been especially successful because the woman who wrote the proposal for managing feral cats had a very good work history with the people involved in approving the program. She was able to identify underlying concerns about the program and address them.

Establishing good relationships with the local government (city councils, mayors, etc.) can be helpful, as can be seeking out people in high places who are cat lovers. The founders of a program for cats in New Jersey identified council members who could help with an ordinance that would get the city to subsidize local spay/neuter programs; the group then spent time educating them on cat problems and solutions. Their efforts got a boost when one of the council members was helped with a rat problem by a wandering cat. The Texas A&M University program had support from the physical plant department—the unit responsible for dealing with cats on campus until the managed colony program was put into place—once the colony program was presented to a cat lover in a high position in the unit.

A veterinarian active in local veterinary politics can be especially useful as a well-regarded and well-known member of the veterinary community and as someone connected to the media, the government, and other important groups. One or two designated people should deal directly with veterinarians to decrease confusion and improve relationships.

There will be times when residents and cat feeders resist moving beyond talking about problems to actually taking action. They may lack knowledge of or genuine concern for the cats. In some circumstances, elderly or disabled cat feeders may be physically unable to participate in trapping; having a small cadre of trappers who can trap at those sites will help this subset of caretakers.

It is crucial to make volunteers feel good about their accomplishments. Thank-you notes should be sent to veterinarians and shelter professionals who participate in group programs, and these professionals should be publicly acknowledged whenever possible. All volunteers should be praised and supported. Criticism about or from volunteers, including veterinarians and animal shelters, should be addressed immediately by a group leader. This person should set the tone and the example for the group by being positive and by providing constructive comments in a private setting. The group leader should talk to troublemakers and ask them to leave the group if necessary. Some groups have strict guidelines for behavior, particularly if surgery or handling the cats is involved. For the safety of group members, the well-being of the cats, and the reputation of the group, these guidelines must be followed. Anyone who violates these guidelines should be asked not to participate. Monitoring volunteers can be especially difficult when there is no central physical location for the activities. Sometimes it is more effective for the group to encourage someone with philosophies in conflict with the group's mission to look for another organization with which to become involved.

Well-established groups face a different set of issues, including keeping or modifying the focus of the group, preventing burnout, and maintaining long-time members as valuable participants. For example, once a high-volume spay/neuter clinic has been running for a time, the group must decide whether continuing the program is enough or whether the group should develop educational materials, actively seek out others to reproduce the program, expand internationally, etc. Keeping people excited and preventing burnout is a problem that most animal welfare, rescue, or protection groups face. The extent of the problem and prevention method will depend on the type of program and the intensity of the time commitment. Typically, this problem is addressed by actively recruiting new volunteers and organizers to redistribute the work, rotate the organizational responsibilities, and bring in new ideas and perspectives. Refocusing on a more manageable mission also may help. If enough new people have joined, expanding the group's services can keep existing members enthusiastic by channeling their energies into new areas. Refocusing can also lead to dissatisfaction, however; original members may distance themselves if the focus of the group changes dramatically. Often groups will add new activities rather than abandon original activities. For example, a group might begin by trapping and sterilizing feral cats, then develop adoption and fostering as a new focus. People whose main interest is in feral cat caretaking may feel excluded by the funding and support given to the new programs. If the original mission really does become obsolete, the group can gracefully "retire" original members or help them orient themselves to the new focus. But it is rare for the original mission to be so successfully accomplished that such people are truly no longer needed. It is important, therefore, to retain these members by keeping their original priorities in mind and valuing their contributions.

7.3 Working with Private-Practice Veterinarians

Any feral cat caretaker or group must work with at least one supportive veterinarian. The Forgotten Felines manual has examples of letters, agreements, and procedures it uses with private-practice veterinarians. Protocols are established with each practitioner, including the number of cats to be treated and times for pick-up and drop-off. Operation Catnip's manual includes advice on how to be prepared and professional in any presentation to potential participating veterinarians. Spay/USA has a network of veterinarians around the country who will provide subsidized or low-cost sterilization, usually at not more than $35 for cats. The program's materials also have advice for recruiting veterinarians.

Establishing a relationship with a veterinarian prior to the onset of trapping is crucial. Written arrangements on the number of cats, scheduling, type of trap or carrier, record keeping, and costs and payment terms should be determined in advance. A veterinarian must earn a living and likely has other clients who are seeking discounted care. He or she may not feel comfortable with the level of discount requested by the group under these circumstances. Some veterinarians have a limited amount of time to contribute, either during clinic hours or afterwards. Veterinarians in multi-person practices may have greater flexibility to schedule their time and therefore may be more willing to participate. One-person practices often have limited time for surgeries and may have limited housing for cats.

One attraction for veterinarians who participate in monthly high-volume spay/neuter programs is the limited time and preparation required on their part. These programs usually use a humane society clinic, and the feral-cat organization does all the preparation, planning, and staffing. No staff or equipment is required from the veterinarian. He or she is not dealing with the public, is appreciated, and is treated well. The veterinary supervisor for the Berkeley, California-based Fix Our Ferals program, modeled after the Feral Cat Coalition program in San Diego, California, convinced additional veterinarians to work for the program for these reasons. Occasionally, a veterinary facility is used; in such cases, the veterinarian has made more of a commitment to the program's goals and objectives.

Established nonprofit groups and veterinarians agree that it is crucial to have one or two people who serve as liaisons between the group and the veterinarians. All trapping and health care should be approved and scheduled by these people. This will reduce the likelihood of conflict between the caretakers and the veterinarians since services will have been pre-arranged. If questions arise, the liaison can mediate and prevent veterinarians and caretakers from spending time debating what should be done or what will be paid for.

It is a good idea to encourage participating veterinarians to educate their staffs about the differences between treating feral and socialized cats. Material from such organizations as Alley Cat Allies (see Appendix D), the SF SPCA's Feral Cat Assistance Program, and the Universities Federation for Animal Welfare (Universities Federation for Animal Welfare 1995) or information such as *Understanding and Controlling Feral Cat Populations* (Slater 2001) can be helpful. Consulting with other veterinarians who have experience with feral cats can be useful as well. General information on handling feral cats—such as confining cats in escape-proof carriers or traps, one cat per container—is available from the SF SPCA and similar organizations.

Julie Levy, D.V.M., of Operation Catnip in Florida, suggests that groups make sure that everyone involved honors written agreements with participating veterinarians and that, if problems occur, the veterinarians are dealt with honestly and openly. Groups should recognize the importance of the veterinarians' help by making client referrals, offering recognition in newsletters and the press, and presenting awards and gifts.

7.4 Creating High-Volume Subsidized Feral Cat Spay/Neuter Clinics

The vets should be involved at the highest level of the organization and should be treated like gods. Without the vet community, we are just a lot of well-intended folks feeding cats.

—A feral cat spay/neuter clinic volunteer

This sentiment is echoed by many of the people who run successful feral cat programs of all sorts, not just spay/neuter clinics. But is it especially important for the clinics because of the relatively large number of veterinarians needed to make these clinics successful in the long-term. The mission for these clinics is to sterilize as many feral cats as possible to reduce the population. The clinics are generally not associated with an animal shelter program; most are stand-alone, once-a-month clinics. The Feral Cat Coalition (FCC) in San Diego, California, established in 1992 by veterinarians and caretakers, is often pointed to as the model for this type of program. Many clinics in California and elsewhere are based on the FCC's guidelines and materials. Operation Catnip in North Carolina (established in 1996) and Florida (established in 1998) uses local veterinary college facilities for their clinics. They have informal connections to the veterinary colleges' resources, including students and veterinarians in graduate training who want to keep their surgical skills sharp. The Operation Catnip manual is a thorough and well-laid-out guide to its program. Julie Levy stresses the need to focus any such program by exploring some initial questions: (1) what kinds of cats will be included in the clinics; (2) will the program take the form of a high-volume, intermittently scheduled "spay day" or a more continuous flow of animals to the veterinary hospital; (3) who will provide facilities and equipment; (4) who will be on the board of directors; (5) where is the funding coming from; and (6) assuming the goal is to decrease numbers of feral cats, how will it track success or failure. As an example of a program grappling with the last question, the Feral Cat Spay/Neuter Program in Lynnwood, Washington, is able to track numbers in the five shelters that will be most affected by its high-volume spay/neuter clinics because Washington State tracks animal shelter data.

In 1997 114 cats were sterilized. By the end of 2001, 3,914 cats had been sterilized in the program.

Because of funding limitations, each clinic was capped at 100 cats in 2001. Over time, the group hopes that this program can document the effect on the number of stray cats entering the facilities, two of which are animal care and control facilities.

7.5 Spreading the Word

National networks can be effective at pulling together people, resources, and expertise. Alley Cat Allies and Spay/USA have networks that provide links for people around the country. Informal networking—visiting a program similar to one a group is interested in developing, for example—can be helpful to avoid re-inventing the wheel and to access suppliers of food, equipment, and pharmaceuticals. Groups should create partnerships with shelters, animal care and control programs, subsidized spay/neuter programs, veterinary medical associations, and local businesses.

Networking can include bringing local agencies together or identifying existing resources that may be helpful. A grant provided to New Jersey residents funds a program that provides sterilization of feral cats, maintains files on active caretakers and colonies, and lists trap resources (who will lend, rent, or sell), veterinarians (listed by county), prices for sterilization, maps, and "cat captains"—people who can offer advice, trapping assistance, places to hold cats temporarily, or fund-raising information. In the first year, ninety caretakers became part of the program, each becoming eligible to receive up to $350 to pay for sterilization of a large colony.

Publishing and distributing materials—brochures, fliers, press releases —will increase awareness of the group and its mission. Brochures can be placed in veterinary offices, pet stores, feed stores, and other locations that people interested in animals may frequent. Fliers can be put up in neighborhoods, left on doors, or posted in schools and businesses. Web sites, manuals, printed guidelines, and information sheets can also be used to disseminate information. Local newspaper stories and television and radio spots can generate phone calls, e-mails, and letters—although not all will be supportive. Booths at local fairs; cat, dog, and horse shows; and, when nearby, open houses at veterinary colleges and related animal programs can provide opportunities to distribute written materials, show videos, and speak with people face-to-face. At the annual open house at the College of Veterinary Medicine at Texas A&M University, which draws thousands of people from all over the state, the booth for the campus feral cat program was staffed by a person available to answer questions, had a videotape running about the program, and included brochures on the group and general information on feral cats.

Established groups should consider working with less experienced or knowledgeable caretakers or feeders to raise the standard of care of the cats in their neighborhoods. This will improve the lifestyle of the cats and increase the legitimacy of the organization and cat caretakers.

A written proposal can help convince business and property owners that a feral cat program will benefit themselves and the community. The document should outline a brief history of the problem; explain how TTVAR-M will solve the problem; identify who is responsible for what; and address any specific concerns expressed in the past. One or two well-written pages should be enough. Materials on TTVAR-M or case studies of successful programs may also be helpful.

7.6 Managing Colonies

The Process

A colony management program must have reliable feeders, a safe environment with appropriate shelter, and veterinary assistance. A set of guidelines from Alley Cat Allies *(Feral Cat Population Control)* lists seven steps to achieve these goals: (1) assessing the initial situation (number of cats and feeders, health of cats, suitability of location); (2) setting up regular feeding schedules; (3) planning for which cats will remain on the site; (4) arranging for veterinary care (surgery, testing, vaccination, and ear-tipping); (5) trapping the cats; (6) placing kittens or tame adults in homes; and (7) maintaining the colony (feeding, watering, providing shelter, trapping new cats, and removing any ill or injured cats). San Francisco's Feral Cat Assistance Program, Forgotten Felines of Sonoma County, and the Doris Day Animal League have overlapping guidelines. The latter two programs support testing for FeLV and FIV, obtaining written consent from the landowner, and providing oversight by an established animal protection group to ensure that cats are trapped humanely and given appropriate health care. The groups emphasize the importance of maintaining medical records and trapping data. Forgotten Felines has a comprehensive manual, *A Guide to the TTVAR-M Method of Feral Cat Control;* Operation Catnip and other established groups provide similar guidelines. Another option for groups to consider is placing information signs at locations where cats historically have been abandoned. Signs can warn cat owners of any local penalties for abandonment and provide alternative suggestions for where to turn for assistance.

In Honolulu, a group of city and county employees decided to do something about the cats living in five city- and county-owned locations. Working with the Hawaiian Humane Society, the group sterilized 127 cats and placed 45 for adoption during a four-year period. It took two to four years to trap and sterilize the feral cats in the five locations and stabilize their numbers. Sixty-two cats were trapped and sterilized in the first four months. Such success would have been extremely difficult without a subsidized (free) spay/neuter program and help from experienced cat trappers and caretakers. Continued abandonment and influx of stray cats has required ongoing capture and adoption. The group's short but data-filled newsletter keeps members, government officials, and interested caretakers updated on progress and provides a forum for ideas.

Record Keeping

Establishing a level of care—in writing, if possible—for all cat caretakers in the group can prove helpful if the group is trying to work with other organizations. Such standards reflect the group's commitment and organizational sophistication.

Keeping track of the cats in the colony in some written format can be helpful in documenting the effectiveness of the TTVAR-M approach. Alley Cat Allies (Appendix D), Forgotten Felines of Sonoma County, and Neponset Valley Humane Society, among others, use a variety of record-keeping formats. Basic information to include for each cat is (1) name and description (possibly with a photo); (2) sex (and neuter status if not yet sterilized); (3) approximate age; (4) FeLV/FIV test results; (5) vaccination data and rabies certificate; (6) health problems and treatments; and (7) final outcome if the cat disappears or dies or is euthanized or adopted.

Basic information on each colony should include (1) the location; (2) the date that management began; (3) the names and phone numbers of caretakers; (4) the numbers of adults and kittens in the colony at the onset of management; (5) the numbers remaining after all are sterilized and tame adults and kittens are removed; and (6) the veterinarian(s) or program(s) providing sterilization and other health care.

Trapping

Care is needed whenever trapping is undertaken in areas where owned cats may be mingling with abandoned and feral cats. This is especially likely in apartment complexes and mobile home parks. Although some communities require a collar or tag so outdoor owned cats may be easily identified, not all do so, nor do all owners comply. Before trapping, post notices alerting cat owners to trapping dates and be sure that the property owner or manager knows what is being done and why. Group members may also want to talk to neighbors and residents who show interest in the cats to determine which cats may be owned. One group suggests placing a collar on friendly cats with a message about the program and a phone number so an owner can make contact before trapping begins.

Many established feral cat programs, including Forgotten Felines, Alley Cat Allies, SF SPCA, the Neponset Valley Humane Society, and Operation Catnip offer guidelines, videotapes, and suggestions for trapping. The HSUS has a handout on live-trapping feral cats (see Appendix C). Individuals with experience may be available for consultation. Humane traps in several different sizes are manufactured by various vendors (see The HSUS's annual *Shelter Pages* directory, in Resources, for a listing of companies that manufacture or distribute such traps). Traps should be cleaned and identified in some way before use. Ideally, they should not be left unattended, since frightened cats can injure themselves and may be vulnerable to other animals and people. Traps should not be placed in the sun, and cats should not be trapped in very cold weather (below forty degrees Farenheit). Traps should be covered as soon after a cat enters as possible to help quiet the animal. In some cases, covering the trap while waiting for the cat to enter will help. The floor of the trap should be covered with newspaper, hay or other plant material, cloth, or carpet cut to fit. Tuna, sardines, and fish-flavored cat food are common baits, but for some cats mackerel, roast beef, cheese, catnip, fried chicken, or cat toys are irresistible. A portion of the bait should be placed near the trap entrance to entice the cat to approach it. Cats should not be fed a meal at their regular feeding station before trapping to increase the likelihood that they will enter the trap to eat. Some experts recommend that traps should be cleaned and disinfected between cats, while others believe that a trap can be left as is from use to use.

Nursing females pose a special problem; if they are captured without their kittens, the kittens may starve, but if they are released to nurse their kittens, they may become too wary to be trapped again. Ideally, the caretaker will know which cats are nursing and where the kittens may be so that traps are not set where these mothers are likely to be caught. Trapping should not take place during the prime season for nursing kittens, usually late spring and summer.

For cats wary of humane traps, there are several strategies. One is to use a trap that can be tripped by the trapper instead of the cat. At least one vendor of cat-trapping equipment sells such a system. (The SF SPCA video describes how to modify a standard humane trap so that it can be tripped only by the trapper.) Another strategy is to use homemade or commercially available traps made of Plexiglas and plastic so that there are no metal or other visual barriers for trap-shy cats; such traps may also be tripped by the trapper. This kind of trap can be helpful in catching whole litters of kittens, since the trapper can wait until all the kittens are inside before closing the door. A third strategy is netting, which can work if the cat will allow the person to get relatively close or is in a confined space. Some special expertise is needed, however, and netting is more hazardous to the human and more stressful for the cat than the other methods. Feeding the cats for several days in the traps before setting them is often helpful.

Feeding and Sheltering

It is generally agreed that regularly scheduled daily or twice daily feeding is best for feral cats. Such a schedule habituates the cats to coming to a location at a particular time, which allows the caretaker to observe current colony residents and check for any new arrivals. In many locations, feeding areas can become soiled, drawing negative attention to the cats and attracting rodents, raccoons, and other wild animals to the site. In such situations a hidden feeding station may be helpful. If ants, other insects, or rodents are a problem, cat food should only be made available for a limited time at each feeding. Feeding bowls should be picked up and removed, not left to litter the area. Usually a dry, name-brand commercial cat food is the most economical choice and provides adequate nutrition. Some caretakers make or mix their own food or use canned food for part of the diet. Canned and other wet foods will spoil quickly in warm weather, though. Water should always be provided at the feeding area.

The type of shelter needed by the cats will vary, depending on climate and location. In colder climates, insulated, well-designed shelters are crucial to protect the cats from the elements if other buildings or barns are not usable. In warmer climates, shelters should provide protection from the wind and rain. Plans for shelters are available from many programs, including Alley Cat Allies, Forgotten Felines, the SF SPCA (via its videotape), and the Feral Cat Coalition. A variety of creative options have been used to protect cats, however, and the materials can often be obtained as donations from lumber or home-and-garden stores.

7.7 Working with Animal Care and Control Agencies and Humane Societies

A good working relationship with local animal care and control agencies can help protect cats who are not yet managed in any systematic way. If animal care and control agencies refer those who are willing to help solve cat problems to the grass-roots group, the group can bring in new caretakers and move more feral cats into managed colonies. When people surrendering feral cats to local shelters or calling about a mother cat and kittens are put in touch with the local group, the group can work with them to have the cats trapped and neutered or tamed. Grass-roots groups can develop basic information on trapping, managing colonies, or taming kittens and can ask the humane society or animal care and control agency to distribute this information to their clients.

Being well informed on larger issues will improve a group's credibility and ability to work with others. These issues include the impact of feral cats on wildlife and birds, public health concerns, and the limitations imposed on some humane societies and animal care and control agencies by their employers, finances, or facilities. Grass-roots groups should remember that some humane societies and animal care and control agencies have several constituencies. They should remember, too, that public health agencies and animal care and control agencies have their own missions and may have laws and ordinances to enforce (Handy 2001).

Animal Shelter Approaches

CHAPTER

8

The term "animal shelter" includes facilities operated by nonprofit humane societies, humane societies with animal sheltering contracts, and public animal care and control agencies with sheltering facilities. In addition to providing general education on responsible pet ownership, animal shelters may be involved in feral cat issues in a variety of ways. For example, they may not have an open-door policy for cats, due to a lack of legal authority and/or funding, which can lead to cats being abandoned or killed in less-than-humane ways. They may accept feral cats and have to euthanize them, sometimes in large numbers. They may have to hold feral cats in the same place that they hold socialized cats, leading to safety issues for staff and potential overcrowding and other cat welfare issues. They may have fewer potential homes available for shelter cats because residents instead have taken in feral kittens or somewhat socialized adult cats directly from the streets. More positively, they may provide services that feral cat caretakers can use to help care for their colonies, or they may be actively partnering with feral cat caretakers and organizations.

All shelters should learn about the sources and disposition of cats in their communities. They should determine the total number of cats coming into the shelter, including the numbers of unsocialized cats, kittens, and strays, and make note of problem areas. Keeping accurate records, broken down by number of cats and dogs (further broken down to adults/puppies and adults/kittens is even better), will facilitate collecting information and make it easy to track changes with time. These data will also allow the shelter to determine where resources are currently going and where they might be most usefully directed. As one shelter director said, "Not all the cats we should be helping are in our building."

If shelters are holding feral cats, particularly in large numbers, housing them can be a challenge. One approach is to house the cats in standard cat cages and use various types of restraint while the staff clean the cage and feed the cats. This is stressful for both staff and cats.

The second option is to house cats in standard cages outfitted with a specially designed feral cat box. The box, designed by animal shelter professionals who handle large numbers of feral cats, is sold by several vendors. The front door slides down from the top to transfer cats from a humane trap into the cage and a swivel side-door can be closed to contain the cat in the box or left open to allow the cat to hide in the box. Holes on the sides of the box allow personnel to inject a cat with an anesthetic agent while the cat is inside.

The third approach is to create group housing areas for cats. A successful group-housing model has been used by the Fort Wayne (Indiana) Department of Animal Care and Control. Each housing unit has a series of fold-down shelves built up the sides; food and litter boxes are on the floor. Three adjacent housing units are used, with cats trapped on two or three sequential days going into the same unit so that by the end of the week the cats in the first unit have satisfied their mandated holding period and will be removed, so that the process of filling the units begins all over again. Cats that, after a "cooling off" period, are clearly socialized are removed and made available for adoption. After the holding period mandated by law has ended for the last cat trapped in that housing unit, the cats are netted, starting from the top shelves down, by specially trained staff and removed for euthanasia. This type of housing requires more renovation of existing facilities, but it can be successful in areas where large numbers of feral cats are held for a long time.

As mentioned previously, shelters can provide several services to caretakers. They can include (1) loaning or renting traps; (2) assisting with trapping; (3) microchipping and maintaining a registry of microchip numbers; (4) providing subsidized spay/neuter vouchers; (5) providing in-house subsidized spay/neuter programs (some without cost to the caretakers); (6) returning ear-tipped and/or microchipped cats to caretakers; (7) coordinating feral colony management; (8) accepting tame cats from managed colonies for adoption; (9) providing foster homes and adoption for feral kittens; (10) providing education workshops on feral cat care and management; and (11) serving as a central repository for information and experts on feral cats.

Shelters can also identify and coordinate adoptions at adoption sites other than the shelter facility. These sites may include places of business such as pet supply stores, veterinary clinics, feed stores, or non-animal-related concerns. If the feral-cat group provides the cages and transportation and potential adopters are identified—but not approved—at these sites, the final adoption interview, paperwork, and animal transfer can be done elsewhere. This limits any inconvenience to the business itself.

If shelter staff are aware that ear-tipped or ear-notched cats are part of an ongoing management program, such cats can be reunited with their caretakers and avoid euthanasia. An organized group should have one or two people available for shelter personnel to contact if an ear-tipped cat comes into the shelter. The group then is responsible for finding the appropriate caretaker, based on the location and description of the cat. If feral cats are being microchipped, caretakers can be identified from the microchip number and contacted directly by the shelter.

Many shelters have found that forming partnerships with existing feral cat organizations is an effective way to incorporate managed colonies into the community cat effort. Some of the larger and best known of these programs include the Neponset Valley Humane Society and the SF SPCA. Another is the MHS, which takes in 5,000 animals per year and euthanizes 800, 600 of whom are cats. About one of every three cats is feral. The humane society provides free sterilization, microchipping, testing for FeLV and FIV (and euthanasia of positive cats), vaccinations, and tattooing on the female incisions. It does not ear-tip cats. In recent years the number of feral cats has decreased as several long-term colonies have been successfully managed and stabilized.

Innovative programs to educate owners and keep pets in their original homes are nothing new to animal shelter professionals. Programs that emphasize feline biology and behavior, creative ways to make cats happy indoors or in enclosures, and humane trapping, among others, are needed. The Wake County (North Carolina) Animal Shelter, in partnership with local veterinary students, developed a program for new pet owners in 1999 (see Resources). The sessions include basic information and provide the pet owner with ongoing contact with the students for additional questions.

Veterinary Involvement

Education is a key contribution by veterinarians in dealing with the feral cat problem (Slater 2001). Veterinarians are uniquely equipped to educate clients about pet overpopulation, the importance of sterilization, choosing an appropriate pet, normal cat behavior, alternatives for pets that must be given up, and considerations for outdoor cats (Christiansen 1998). Veterinarians also can educate feral cat caretakers. Handouts on quarantine for new cats and kittens coming into a household (why, when, and where and how to clean and disinfect); information on the types, causes, treatments, and prevention of common infectious diseases; how and why to keep treatment records; and medication dosage rates for cats and kittens are all helpful for caretakers' efforts.

Veterinarians often become involved in caring for or sterilizing feral cats as a service to the community. Some veterinarians become involved because of their unwillingness to euthanize a healthy animal, because they have information that trapping and euthanasia are not effective in a particular area, or because they want to investigate other options. Others get involved through their clients.

As part of his or her practice, a veterinarian may provide spay/neuter and health care services for established or new clients who are caring for feral cats. Veterinary hospitals may accept vouchers or coupons for subsidized spay/neuter of feral and owned cats. The veterinarians also may volunteer to help established feral cat grass-roots groups. They may act as surgeons for a large-scale feral cat surgery program, such as that of the Feral Cat Coalition or Operation Catnip, provide prepubertal spay/neuter (beginning as young as eight weeks old)—a crucial service—test for FeLV and FIV, and give advice on infectious disease control. All feral cats should be vaccinated for rabies if they live in an area where rabies can occur.

Veterinarians can work for organizations that provide subsidized sterilizations, such as humane societies; practices with an emphasis on spaying and neutering; or clinics, including mobile spay/neuter vans. Some may start their own spay/neuter clinic. Members of the National Spay/Neuter Coalition can provide advice on establishing a clinic, as can many existing clinics, such as Dr. Marvin Mackie's Animal Birth Control hospitals in Los Angeles and John A. Caltabiano's TEAM (Tait's Every Animal Matters) van in Westport, Connecticut (see Resources). The TEAM van functions six days a week and averages 35 cats per day (at $39 per cat, including vaccinations). In its first eighteen months, it sterilized 12,500 cats, including many feral cats. While donations are solicited for additional programs, the unit itself is self-supporting. Many other resources are available on the Internet, from the Operation Catnip manual, and from other organizations.

9.1 Handling Feral Cats in the Practice Setting

Dealing with feral cat caretakers individually or as part of organized groups requires that the veterinarian determine a personal comfort level for services and health care. Some caretakers may offer the veterinarian the opportunity to see their colonies and observe the level of care provided. Caretakers are usually extremely dedicated to their cats and can be persistent when trying to obtain care for them. A veterinarian offering discounted services should keep a record of the full cost of the care provided to track what is being spent on this part of the practice. Veterinarians working with feral cat caretakers emphasize the need to be empathetic, have flexibility, and avoid judgmental attitudes. Some caretakers, like some other clients, may try to take advantage of a veterinarian's compassion and generosity. They may also "test" a veterinarian by bringing in a few cats for care before revealing that they care for hundreds. For these reasons, a veterinarian should establish a personal philosophy for care of feral cats prior to interacting with caretakers. Putting agreed terms in writing may also help avoid friction later.

Providing feral cats with a fifteen- to thirty-minute "cooling off" period after they arrive at the veterinarian's office and before undergoing any procedures will reduce stress and may improve the smoothness of the anesthetic induction. Cats can be kept in their traps for the duration of their stay in the clinic (which is usually less than twenty-four hours) to prevent escape. If cats are to be transferred to different housing, the transfer should always be done in a closed room with a solid ceiling (cats can go through a suspended tile-type ceiling with great speed). Most cat cages used in practices are poorly suited to hold feral cats, especially for any length of time, and the cats may be difficult to remove or restrain. (See chapter 8 for information on a recently developed box better suited for handling feral cats.)

Squeeze cages designed to fit against the end of humane traps are manufactured or sold by humane trap companies. These wire squeeze cages allow the handler to press the cat against the side of the cage for restraint prior to giving injections. Cats also may be restrained by inserting a comb-like, slide-in divider near the bottom of a wire humane trap above the cat after the trap has been tipped on its end. The teeth of the divider slide between the wires on one side and out the other side, forming a temporary wall. Such cages and traps present the smallest risk to personnel. Some personnel are adept at catching and restraining feral cats with gloves, towels, and/or blankets, but because these methods are more risky to personal safety and more stressful for the cats, they are not recommended.

Feral cats have unknown medical histories, and in some areas, high rates of respiratory disease. Keeping them in a separate area of the clinic will reduce the spread of diseases.

9.2 Anesthesia and Surgery

Anesthetic protocols for feral cats are usually different from those appropriate for pet cats, since an injectable anesthetic combination to immobilize the cat for examination, euthanasia, and/or surgery is usually required. Several such combinations are being used, some of which provide better analgesia and relaxation than others. Combinations of ketamine and xylazine or tiletamine-zolazepam, with or without butorphanol, provide good relaxation and pain control with reasonable safety for the cat.

A physical examination can be performed and the sex determined once the cat is anesthetized. Basic health care is different for this population of cats than for many pets. Internal and external parasites and infectious diseases rarely seen in indoors-only, well-cared-for cats may be common in some feral cat colonies. These cats have unknown health histories and cannot be examined prior to anesthesia, so it is important to remind the caretakers that there may be an increased risk of complications during anesthesia and surgery. Furthermore, since a cat may have a serious health problem that makes it risky to return to the colony, caretakers should be reminded that euthanasia, rather then sterilization, may be necessary (Slater 2001). The criteria for euthanasia should be determined as part of the initial agreement, but because of the limited ability to provide ongoing treatment, difficulties in re-trapping some cats, and colony lifestyle, the decision to euthanize a feral cat may need to be made sooner than it would be for a pet cat.

Following examination and testing (if performed), the cats are sterilized using absorbable skin sutures or intradermal closure for spays, with tissue glue used as needed to close the incision completely. A debate regarding the strengths and weaknesses of the flank incision versus the ventral abdominal incision for females is ongoing, but complications using either method are extremely rare and the surgeon should choose. For the flank approach, the surgeon makes the incision on the cat's side, behind the rib cage, rather than down the middle of the belly. (A videotape describing how to perform flank incisions is available from Alley Cat Allies.) The argument for flank incisions is that evisceration is prevented if the closure fails since the incision is higher on the body wall. The flank incision also has clear benefits when spaying recently nursing mothers; mammary gland tissue makes the traditional ventral approach and closure difficult. An argument against flank incisions is that reaching the ovary on the side opposite the incision can be difficult. The flank approach also cannot be used for pregnant females since the uterus and fetuses do not fit easily through the incision and access to the ovaries is difficult.

Before or after surgery, cats should be vaccinated and ear-tipped (or ear-notched with a V-shaped notch). Ear-tipping involves the removal of one centimeter from the tip of one ear, usually the left (Cuffe et al. 1983), and may provide a more clear silhouette than ear-notching. For programs with well-established ear-tipping protocols, the right ear may be done for males and the left for females. This may be difficult to remember and implement in some settings, however, especially if cats are ear-tipped before spay/neuter surgery. Blunt scissors, crushing with a hemostat and then using a scalpel, or laser surgery can all be used for ear tipping. Homeostasis with cautery, pressure, or a styptic powder is important to avoid bleeding or scarring, which can distort the distinctive silhouette (Cuffe et al. 1983). Ear-tipping is the internationally recognized method to identify a cat who has been sterilized and is designed to be seen from a distance. Although some people are concerned with the aesthetics of this procedure, ear-tipping prevents cats from being trapped repeatedly to check for their sterilization status. The Royal College of Veterinary Surgeons approved this approach many years ago (Cuffe et al. 1983; Remfrey 1996). Cats are generally held for twenty-four to forty-eight hours after surgery (females are held longer than males) by the veterinarian or caretaker before being returned to the trapping site.

9.3 Alternatives to Surgical Sterilization

In general, a permanent, relatively low-risk, inexpensive form of sterilization is ideal and, at this point, it usually takes the form of spaying or neutering (Mahlow and Slater 1996). The expense and veterinary expertise required and the logistics of trapping, transporting, and returning cats to the colony, however, have made the idea of an alternative attractive. Vasectomizing males so that the females become pseudopregnant has been suggested and occasionally used (Herron and Herron 1972; Norsworthy 1975; Kendall 1979). Unfortunately, there is limited data on efficacy and long-term effects on the females, and it requires surgery, although only for some males. It does not decrease annoying cat behaviors such as spraying, fighting, yowling, and roaming and requires that the male cat stay in the colony, remain alive, and continue to service the females. That said, fewer animals need to be trapped and undergo surgery. In isolated areas, with little turnover of cats, vasectomies may be a useful alternative to spay/neuter.

Support for this approach is purely anecdotal. One golf course owner in New England vasectomized the one clearly dominant male cat in the company of thirteen females who had litters on his property every year. For the eight years that the cat was alive and vasectomized, only one or two litters were born each year. In another short-term project, all male cats in a Texas trailer park with a history of unwanted kittens were trapped and vasectomized. The following spring, animal control reported that no kittens were seen.

Medical control of feral cat populations has not been well evaluated. It is neither permanent and nor inexpensive. Megasterol acetate, a progestin used as a contraceptive for dogs, is not commonly used in cats because of potentially severe long-term side effects. Sold as Ovaban in the United States, it is available only from veterinarians. Published reports on its use in feral cats are scarce. One paper reports using a dosage of one tablet (5 mg) once a week for four weeks and then half a tablet once weekly (Remfry 1978). The dose was wrapped in minced meat and given individually to each cat. Dosing was continued for ten months until the cats had to be removed and euthanized. Although six of the seven females did not always receive their dose, five of them did not reproduce. The difficulties and cost of dosing each cat are not inconsequential. One Pennsylvania colony of eight cats is managed using 2.5 mg doses of megasterol acetate once weekly for each cat. The caretaker reported not seeing a litter in two years. One practical use for megasterol acetate is for female cats who will come to a feeding station but cannot be trapped. This limits, from an economic standpoint, the number of cats treated and may be an option if preventing kittens is of primary importance. One colony in Vermont has two wary females who cannot be trapped but have been on megasterol acetate for two years without producing a litter.

Drugs that cause abortion midway through pregnancy have also been suggested. The one that has been used on feral cats is a prolactin inhibitor called cabergoline (Jochle and Jochle 1993). Even at low doses, it is expensive and not readily available in the United States. Given too late in the pregnancy, the kittens are born normally, but the mother cannot produce milk and fails to care for the kittens. For these reasons, this type of drug is not recommended. Progress on other non-surgical methods of sterilization is slowly being made. The Alliance for Contraception in Cats and Dogs *(http://www.vetmed.vt.edu/accd/)* is a good place to watch for future developments.

Government Involvement

10.1 Animal Care and Control Agencies

Much of the information in chapter 8 is applicable to public animal care and control agencies that have their own shelters. Because such programs are so diverse, the approaches and programs need to be tailored carefully to the situation. Many programs have a limited number of officers, may have a history of focusing on dog problems, or may or may not have to enforce ordinances. The traditional role of animal control agencies is to protect the public from animals through such programs as sterilization, vaccination, complaint investigation, enforcement of ordinances, and quarantine and through such duties as cruelty investigations, animal rescue, humane education, shelters for adoptions, returning pets to owners, and mediation. Animal care and control usually handles cat nuisance complaints—yowling and fighting, digging in gardens, dirty foot prints on cars, spraying on homes, bites—and concerns about sick or injured cats. Some animal control programs and duties may be in conflict with each other, especially when funding is restricted and there is limited awareness of larger animal-related issues in the community. There also may be a tendency to be more reactive than proactive, and many feral cat management solutions require a proactive, long-term approach. Several animal care and control professionals have encouraged animal care and control planners to recognize that what has been done in the past is not accomplishing what the community wants or may be too restrictive for the current problems.

Approaches

It is recommended that animal care and control agencies create written policy statements about pertinent cat-related problems, such as euthanasia in the field, quarantine procedures, and sick or injured animals in the field and in the shelter. These agencies should develop or gain permission to use or modify published material on commonly asked questions and problems, humane handling and trapping of cats and other animals, options for controlling feral cats, and possible solutions for common complaints about feral or free-roaming cats (apart from trapping and removal).

Just as behavior help-lines and specialists are now working with some shelters and agencies to help with common owned-dog and -cat problems, specialists can be enlisted to find solutions to common feral and free-roaming cat complaints. For example, one expert recommends adding a pile of peat moss (which cats prefer as a litter material) in an inconspicuous location in the yard of a caretaker to stop cats from defecating in a complaining homeowner's yard. Peat moss controls odor, and it can be removed and replaced on a monthly basis. The Hawaiian Humane Society has published a brochure that offers tips on ways to discourage cats from coming into a yard, including repellents, deterrents, and surprise devices. For owners whose cats have been trapped by animal control officers in response to complaints, the Hawaiian Humane Society has a card that explains cat behavior, encourages keeping cats indoors, and offers additional information on making the outdoors/indoors transition. The Cat Care Society in Lakewood, Colorado, publishes a brochure for the public on what to do with a homeless cat. The Forsyth County (North Carolina) Department of Animal Control developed a brochure to help citizens with animal problems determine whom to call under what circumstances because the jurisdictions and responsibilities in its area are complex. The brochure also describes the process for reporting cruelty to animals or dog bites and includes safety tips (see the Forsyth County Animal Shelter listing in Resources).

Networking is as important for an animal care and control agency as it is for any other group. It should coordinate and share responsibilities so that organizations complement each other in services and strengths.

Keeping good records is especially important for agencies that are funded by the city or county. Documentation of the numbers and types of complaints received and answered can be an effective tool for leveraging support during the budget review process. Figures showing, for example, the number of police and fire fighters per resident compared to the number of animal control officers per resident can be helpful. Describing the extent and efficacy of programs such as microchipping, lost and found, adoptions, sterilization (of adopted animals), and trap loans can be used to emphasize accomplishments. Animal care and control agencies often spend money directly or indirectly on feral cats through shelters and through their handling of complaints. They should consider reallocating some of these dollars to proactive feral cat-related programs.

An unusual example of a very comprehensive animal care and control program is found in Orange County, Florida. Orange County Animal Care and Control (OCACC) (now Orange County Animal Services) staff had been euthanizing feral cats since 1984 and dealing with nuisance complaints on a daily basis. They were concerned about the frequency of cat euthanasia in their facility and wanted to be proactive in their responses, despite limited staffing and funding. Over several months they planned new programs and modified ordinances. They added breeding restrictions, leash laws, and nuisance provisions and modified the definition of "owner" to someone who allowed an animal on his or her property for more than thirty days with the intent of keeping the animal. Because they were not quite sure how best to handle feral cats, they left specific mention of them out of the ordinance. Once the ordinance was passed, however, they deemed feral cat caretakers to be "breed rescue groups," which had been included. Caretakers who are either individuals or members of unincorporated groups register with the agency and can then take animals from the shelter and receive free sterilization, ear notching, and rabies vaccinations for cats. Care Feline Rescue, a nonprofit organization, came forward to serve as the liaison between the agency and other cat caretakers. Care Feline Rescue established to its satisfaction that OCACC wanted to help and had services to offer, but it also recognized that OCACC had to deal with nuisance cats and that if the organization couldn't deal with the problem, the cats would have to be removed. Care Feline Rescue had to provide education on TTVAR-M to the community so that people didn't complain or think that the cats were abandoned. Care Feline Rescue now receives Orange County Animal Services' nuisance cat complaints, and if TTVAR-M is deemed to be the solution, it takes care of trapping and sterilization. The organization has a staff person who schedules feral cat surgeries. Participants meet three or four times a year to identify problems and solutions. Between the program's beginning in December 1995 and the end of 1999, 3,600 feral cats were sterilized. Of this number, 5 cats continued to present nuisance problems and were removed with the knowledge of the caretakers. Orange County Animal Services has a mobile spay/neuter van for dogs and cats and is currently emphasizing identification for cats to improve the existing 6-percent return-to-owner rate. Despite a growing human population in the community, overall complaints have been leveling off. Cat euthanasia numbers have begun to decrease. The program has been a success because of the commitment, flexibility, and willingness of Orange County Animal Services staff and feral cat caretakers to develop a spirit of cooperation. Continued communication and accepting responsibility were key; if a mistake was made, on either side, it was admitted and resolved.

10.2 Corporate Complexes, Military Bases, and Indian Reservations

Special subsets of the community often have their own regulations on the number of pets permitted, animals running at-large, and/or animal feeding in public areas. They may have an enforcement agency or individual responsible for enforcement separate from the local government. The individual(s) responsible for animal care and control must enforce such regulations, which often makes it difficult or impossible to manage feral cat colonies. In corporate settings, conflicting views and overlapping responsibilities must be addressed among property owners, management, and employees. Some locations may present opportunities for partnerships with grass-roots organizations or local shelters to provide educational materials and assistance with animal-related problems, including feral cat management.

Because of the transient lives of military personnel, abandoned animals may increase the number of free-roaming and feral cats on military installations. On one base, a cat shelter was created. At another site, managed colonies were put into place and tolerated by those in charge. The U.S. Army's policy has typically been to trap and euthanize, in part based on recommendations from The HSUS. In light of recent changes (see Appendix B), the actions of local feral cat caretakers, and the education of military personnel about feral cats, however, managed colonies are becoming increasingly common. Continued attention will likely be paid to cat issues on military property.

Recently, increased veterinary services, including spay/neuter, have been made available on Indian reservations. Control of homeless animals will continue to be a priority in this environment.

Managed Colonies On School Campuses

School campuses are becoming common locations for managed colonies. Cats are often fed and/or watched by students, residents, faculty, and staff, and good habitats may be available. Cats may have been present for a long time, and some sort of trap and euthanize program may have been in place, likely undertaken in response to complaints or bites. Such a haphazard approach—without modifying the habitat—never provides any long-term control or improves the level of care of the cats.

Several colony programs now exist around the country. Some have information on their Web sites, others are known by word of mouth. One colony is at a state school in New England. The campus is a beautiful, geographically isolated area with trees, fields, and both occupied and abandoned buildings. The program began in 1982 when three employees met while feeding cats on campus. Pest control companies had tried to control the numbers of cats by trapping and euthanasia. At the time the employees met, a new effort to trap and remove all the cats was under discussion. This plan had upset staff and residents, many of whom had been feeding the cats for years. Although one person had heard of TTVAR-M programs in England and was eager to try them, the group's resources were limited. It decided to enlist the aid of the regional SPCA to have the cats spayed or neutered and vaccinated before returning them to the school grounds. It told the organization how many cats and kittens it had already placed from the area and that it had received permission from the school administration for its plan. After receiving the SPCA's support, its plan to trap twelve cats was carried out. In letters following the surgeries, the individuals thanked the SPCA for its assistance and described the health of the cats and the pleasure of the residents in having the cats on school grounds.

Since the initial trapping, a few cats have continued to appear on the campus. Most have been tame adults and kittens, some likely wanderers or abandoned animals. The occasional feral cat is seen. The group places tame cats; socializes the kittens; feeds the cats on a regular schedule; maintains shelters (often built by the grounds department); traps and sterilizes new cats; and keeps records of the cats and the care given. A number of the campus cats are over eight years old and two were fourteen-year-old litter mates as of 2001.

Typically at any one time between ten and twenty cats have been living in five to seven colonies around the school. Some of the feral cats eventually became tame enough for the caretakers to offer them for adoption as indoors-only pets.

A second program is located on a California campus. The cats first came to general attention when several cats were accidentally trapped and killed in a building being fumigated. One faculty member wrote a memorandum to the executive vice chancellor indicating that managing the cats on the campus and working closely with the division responsible for the campus facilities would prevent such occurrences in the future. The memo was widely circulated around the campus. Several faculty members, department heads, and a woman familiar with TTVAR-M programs joined with the original letter writer to form a volunteer group. The first meeting between the volunteer group and the facilities maintenance department did not go well because the maintenance staff felt defensive about the deaths of the cats. The group then affiliated itself with a different branch of the administration. The group grew to 125 members, most of whom were students.

Hundreds of cats were on the 400-acre campus. After the group was formed, one veterinarian who had a subsidized spay/neuter clinic provided nearly all the veterinary care. The group developed schedules for feeding stations and reporting mechanisms for identifying new cats. Because of the large initial population, several years passed before there was an obvious decline in the cat population. Funding was provided partly by the school and partly through fund-raising efforts.

When a new head of the maintenance facilities department was hired, he developed a more cooperative relationship with the feral cat group. The faculty advisor for the group estimates that about fifty feral cats remain on campus and that at least twenty socialized cats are removed each year. These socialized cats are especially common at the end of the semester when they are abandoned by students. The campus group works with an adoption organization for placement so that the school has no liability for adopted cats.

As the number of cats has come under control, interest in the group has waned and fewer faculty are involved. During one period, however, an active student participant published a monthly newsletter. Plans are underway to increase the membership again and explore serving as consultants for nearby campuses.

Another program, Aggie Feral Cat Allies of Texas, began in 1998 at Texas A&M University. For at least twenty years, a subdivision of the physical plant department had been responsible for trapping and removing cats when complaints or bites occurred on campus. When several staff and faculty members discovered this, they decided to write a proposal to develop managed colonies, conduct research on the behavior of the cats, and design educational materials for students, staff, and faculty on responsible pet ownership and the link to feral cats. External funding was obtained from a private foundation; the school also provided some funds. The local shelter was consulted to ensure compliance with local ordinances and policies. The number of cats on campus was unknown, but estimates ranged from 100 to 500. The spays and neuters and ear-tipping were performed once a month by senior veterinary students at the campus's veterinary college surgical services as part of their regular rotation. Students from other services in the college provided help with physical examinations, FeLV and FIV testing, and vaccination. Special cages with built-in squeeze mechanisms were designed to minimize risks to staff and students while housing and anesthetizing feral cats. Socialized cats and kittens were taken to the local shelter for adoption or placed privately. Any cat who appeared to be owned was listed in the shelter's lost-and-found book and found-cat advertisements were placed in the local paper. Two graduate students and several staff and faculty members provided oversight for the program, conducted research on the ecology of feral cats on campus, and organized the campus's feeders and feeding stations. After three years, the program had trapped about 200 cats, sterilized and returned about 90 cats, and placed about 70 cats and kittens. The campus educational component included mailings and presentations at various student orientations and functions. Unsterilized feral cats became scarce on campus; most new cats were socialized cats and kittens who were stray or abandoned. By the second year, no kittens were born on campus. To continue the surgical program at the veterinary college, a community group, Brazos Feral Cat Allies, was formed and incorporated in the spring of 2000. This group provides assistance in TTVAR-M in the area and traps cats for subsidized sterilization by the veterinary students.

Future Directions

12

12.1 General Advice

Dealing with feral cat issues requires data, creativity, and good interpersonal skills. Funding must be directed toward partnerships with feral cat caretakers and programs that work. Individuals, organizations, and agencies need to be more proactive in developing interventions and education strategies. Some existing education approaches should be expanded to include accurate, helpful facts and resources about feral cats. National organizations have a variety of roles in finding solutions—the first is to continue to take the lead in recognizing the existence of the problem.

It is wise to avoid sweeping statements about feral cats or organizations that deal with them, since circumstances vary too much from place to place for such statements to be constructive. Discussions about the numbers of individual animals killed by free-roaming cats—even if based on locally accurate data—are nearly always counterproductive. The discussions get bogged down in arguments about the accuracy and applicability of the data and participants lose sight of any common ground.

Every community in the United States should establish a basic animal care and control program. Some communities still have no animal care and control agency, no shelter, and no services of any kind. Owned cats should be confined in some way for their own protection. All outdoor cats should be vaccinated for rabies. Cats adopted from shelters should be sterilized before leaving the facility. It should be possible to define how one owns a cat without being punitive. Owned cats should have some kind of identification to reunite them with their owners if they get lost. Feral cats should be ear-tipped or notched.

12.2 Education and Training

National organizations, local animal care and control agencies, and humane societies can and do provide valuable assistance for both the general public and animal protection professionals. They should also be developing and evaluating different strategies to encourage responsible pet ownership, particularly if the current programs aren't as effective as they could be in a community. Programs must raise awareness of the feral cat problem, so that when people see a cat, owned or not, their first thought is whether the animal is sterilized. If the cat is not owned, they should think about what they could—and should—do about it.

Beyond the usual educational programs, humane societies and animal care and control agencies must distribute information about feral cats that addresses all options. What should people do if they find a feral mother cat and kittens in their bushes? With whom can they talk? Training for animal control officers and shelter personnel should include evaluating various situations, taking advantage of resources available (subsidized sterilization, fostering, adoption, trap availability), and humanely trapping, handling, and euthanizing feral cats. Shelters should consider providing services for feral cat caretakers. In addition to the services already discussed, facilitating workshops for feeders and novice caretakers in conjunction with experienced caretakers could help raise everyone's standard of care and involve more caretakers in the community's efforts.

12.3 Management and Control

Research needs in this area are substantial. If cats must be removed from an area, how well does habitat modification work? What kind of intervention would prevent a colony from developing (if, say, one cat with kittens is abandoned)? What are the optimal procedures for relocation? What percentage of cats survive if relocated as compared to if they remain in established colonies? What changes in hunting behavior occur following sterilization of a colony? Does sterilization and careful location of feeding stations restrict cats' movements so that they have less impact on the local ecosystem? What are the relationships between cats in different environments with different food supplies and other predators in the area?

New forms of permanent sterilization would be a great help for managed colonies, as would an oral rabies vaccine. Bringing technology developed for wildlife to the study of feral cats would require some extensive cooperation, but the technology exists or is being developed that could continuously monitor cats' activity or electronically track patterns of eating at a feeding station.

Record keeping is crucial. To assess whether a program is working, one or two key characteristics (comings, goings, health status, etc.) or numbers must be selected, measured before the program begins, and monitored as the program is implemented. Only by keeping data on important outcomes can a program's success be quantified. Outcomes of interest could include the number of cats in the colony, the number of kittens born in a particular area, the number of feral cats euthanized in a shelter, or the number of complaints received from a given location. The characteristic, number, or outcome should be one of key interest to the group or community, should be likely to be affected by the program of interest, and should be relatively easy to measure objectively. Seek out experts in study design and questionnaire development to help. Get local colleges involved in projects of mutual interest. Cultivate a few key faculty contacts to create an ongoing collaboration.

12.4 Cats and the Human Population

In most cases, data about cats have to be collected at a local or regional level to be accurate and applicable. National or state level data may be needed to plan some types of projects, but unless the state is very small and homogeneous, such information will represent the general situation—not the particular community.

Data on numbers of owned cats and cats in shelters and with rescue groups (if they exist) need to be collected. Data that define the scope of the cat problem and a more detailed evaluation of the sources of feral cats in each community are important for planning and for understanding the situation. The dynamics of the cat population should be better understood. One way of doing so is to use permanent identification of cats such as microchipping, then follow the cats in the community across time to see where they go and what happens to them. This would be time consuming and expensive but could provide valuable insight into cat populations. How could people be reached who have pets but do not see veterinarians or come to animal shelters? Christiansen (1998) has a concise but thorough table on community pet population surveys and their design and conduct.

For any group or organization to develop its programs, it needs information on the human population in the community. Social scientists and marketing professionals use a number of techniques to gain information on people's wants, needs, and opinions, but it is not clear that the best way to ask the most important questions has been determined. Methods should be standardized to determine for each community what constitutes responsible pet ownership so that those ideas can be incorporated in local animal care and control programs. The psychology of cat ownership—why some people form strong bonds with cats and others do not—is poorly studied and could shed some light on the "quasi-owned" cat issue. How do people define pet ownership themselves? Are there patterns to the types of definitions that relate to other lifestyle or pet-owning factors? Some countries, such as Sweden, have relatively few feral cats and few problems relating to them. A cultural comparison could be very enlightening. What are the barriers to keeping pets confined? Are there better methods for veterinarians to work with owners during the early pet-ownership period to improve that relationship?

Conclusions

Feral cats are part of the cat overpopulation problem and exist because of public attitudes and lack of knowledge. They are a problem in most of the United States, as well as in many other countries. Few communities have large-scale, high-visibility programs that deal with feral cats. Many cat caretakers feel threatened or alone. The solution for each community will be different, and in nearly all situations, a combination of approaches will be needed.

Even communities with limited funding or public support, however, can begin to address the problem of feral cats. Existing shelters and animal welfare organizations should recognize the ways in which feral cats contribute to the problems with which they are already grappling. Education and accurate information about feral cats and the options for dealing with them should be made available to the public. Adoption agencies should sterilize all animals prior to releasing the animals from the facility. Shelters must keep records of the numbers of cats and kittens entering and leaving their facilities. Subsidized or low-cost sterilization must be made available, not just to feral cat caretakers but also to those cat owners without the financial means to get their cats sterilized. Sterilization of cats as young as six to eight weeks old should be promoted in any setting where a cat could reproduce: accidentally at a young age, by escaping the house, or as a free-roaming cat. Small groups of caretakers can work together to help themselves and others, provide emotional support, and maximize their ability to solve problems. Becoming incorporated into a nonprofit group may be time consuming and require some financial commitment, but in the long run, it will greatly benefit the group, the cats, and the community.

In communities where basic services are already available, support for feral cat caretakers (including education) and evaluation of options besides "wait and see" or trap and euthanize should be seriously considered as long-term investments. Partnerships with existing grass-roots groups or formation of such groups are also possible next steps to leverage improved care and prevent future generations of feral cats. Formal and informal methods of collecting information on the cat situation and on residents' opinions are crucial to developing the right combination of approaches and obtaining financial support. While there is no one perfect solution for each community, many ideas from other locations may be useful if modified appropriately. The key is communication and cooperation to find the common ground for the many constituencies in each community, including the feral cat caretakers.

Appendix A

Case Study 1: Two Shelters

This case study is on two humane societies with animal care and control contracts that created programs to provide health care and information for feral cats and caretakers. The first program had a partnership with an established grass-roots group but also provided services for any registered caretaker. The second program has an emphasis on high-volume sterilization and health care for feral cats.

Program 1

The first humane society in this case study, in partnership with a grass-roots organization, created a program in April 1995, after eighteen months of negotiation. The program helps members of the grass-roots group manage feral cats in the area. The humane society offered free testing for FeLV/FIV, vaccination, sterilization, use of traps (purchased by the humane society and loaned by the grass-roots group), euthanasia for ill or injured feral cats on request, and advice on obtaining the cooperation of landowners. The program was free, but required registration by caretakers. The registration agreement stated that the caretaker would (1) provide a full-care managed colony (humanely trapping, testing, sterilizing, and returning feral cats and placing tame cats and kittens in homes; providing medical care or euthanasia for ill or injured cats; monitoring and feeding the colony on a regular basis; and identifying of alternate caretakers); (2) complete an annual survey about the colony; and (3) obtain permission from the owner of the land on which the colony is located. The program agreement stipulated that no information about colony locations will be released to the public.

The humane society also offered a variety of programs in the community, including adoptions, animal behavior consultations, obedience classes, field services, cruelty investigations, humane education, dog and cat registration (licensing), pet-loss support groups, subsidized spay/neuter, vaccination and microchipping clinics, a wildlife care center, and information on pets in rental housing.

The grass-roots group has existed, as a nonprofit group, since 1993. It promotes responsible pet ownership, education about proper pet care and health care, adoption, and TTVAR-M for homeless cats. The group emphasizes quality health care and careful, responsible placement of cats. It has a twenty-four-hour phone line that people can call for assistance with funding, moral support, and other purposes. This phone line provides a link between people who are trying to help cats and those with the knowledge and resources to provide them with assistance.

Five years after the program began, there were more than 200 registered colonies and 1,912 cats in the program. More than 1,200 cats had been spayed or neutered through the humane society's clinic, and 736 cats and kittens had been fostered and adopted. Total cat intakes at the humane society had gradually decreased and return-to-owner rates for cats increased. The number of cats euthanized also decreased. (The program ceased operation in this format in 2001.)

Program 2

The second program, begun in 1993, focused on sterilizing as many feral cats as possible. The guidelines provided by the shelter to colony caretakers state, "By working together, we may . . . eliminate the growth of populations of unwanted cats." Caretakers register—at no cost—by signing a release for spay/neuter surgery that also indicates that they will provide basic care and states that the cat being presented for surgery is feral. The guidelines (not requirements) describe the responsibilities of the caretakers, including feeding and monitoring cats, finding homes for any cats who can be socialized, obtaining permission from the landlord/landowner where the colony is located, trapping and sterilizing any new cats, and refraining from disrupting the normal course of the humane society's business. There is no cost for the sterilization and vaccinations. About 1,000 people are registered as caretakers. Because of the high demand, the shelter started two shifts of veterinary staff for sterilizing animals in 1999.

In 1999 the humane society began a series of public meetings about feral cats, with special emphasis on caretakers. They were designed to help maintain communication and develop a deeper appreciation for each participant's needs. Both groups agree that continued communication and cooperation are essential, but the ideal format is still being developed.

The local grass-roots group was the first nonprofit grass-roots organization for feral cats in the region. Working closely with the humane society, the group has found homes for more than 1,000 cats and kittens in its first four years of operation and has trapped and sterilized more than 4,000 cats. Many caretakers work in informal, loosely knit groups.

Special promotions for sterilization and microchipping are provided by the humane society. A 1999 Spay Day offered 500 free cat sterilizations. Routine microchipping and special promotions are having an impact: in 1998, for example, the return-to-owner rate for cats was 4.3 percent. The actual number of cats returned to their owners through microchips was higher than the number of dogs (for 1998, 233 cats and 206 dogs) and the trend was for a continued increase.

In addition to the feral cat program and pre-adoption sterilization and microchipping of all animals, the humane society organizes a subsidized spay/neuter program with surgeries performed by participating local veterinarians. About 10,000 surgeries were performed in the first twelve years of the program. The society's field services department performs cruelty investigations, handles complaints and animal pick-ups, and provides free rides home to lost or stray animals with microchips. Humane education, pet visitation programs, assistance to people with health problems or disabilities, lost and found services, pets-in-housing services for residents of rental and subsidized housing, condominiums, and public housing, and an extensive volunteer network are among the other programs of the humane society.

A humane society goal was to try to increase the return-to-owner rate for cats—it had been about 1 percent. A cat protection law passed in 1995 established that cats could be owned, and that by providing identification, an individual could claim ownership. The law created a minimum holding period for cats of forty-eight hours, with a nine-day holding period for cats carrying any type of identification (collar and tag, microchip, ear tag, or ear-notch). The law mandated sterilization of all outdoor cats over six months old. Violators have the option of having the sterilization performed at the shelter instead of paying the fine. The humane society has been encouraging microchipping of cats, and it charges $5 per cat for the procedure. All microchips in the state are obtained from a single company for uniformity of scanning. Front office staff and animal control officers have a stamp that entitles the bearer to a free spay or neuter for a dog or cat to encourage people with limited resources to sterilize their animals.

In 1994 approximately 7,000 dogs and 20,000 cats entered the shelter; in 1998, 8,000 dogs and 16,000 cats entered the shelter. Cat intake at the shelter decreased from 21,070 in 1995 to 16,246 in 1998. Approximately 9,000 feral cats and 36,000 owned cats were sterilized through humane society programs between 1993 and 1998. Numbers of owner-surrendered, stray, and euthanized cats, older kittens, and newborns had decreased consistently. The return-to-owner rate increased from 1 percent to 4 percent.

In spite of the good work accomplished, some conflict exists between caretakers and the humane society. Shelter workers believe that some caretakers don't want to work with the shelter but do so only to avail themselves of the services provided. Caretakers express skepticism of the humane society's motivation. Potential exists as well for additional conflict with those who provide oversight for parks (where feeding animals is prohibited) and public health officials trying to carry out their missions.

Case Study 2: Two Grass-roots Organizations

The following two grass-roots organizations manage feral cats as their primary goal. The success of the first group has been made possible by a series of fortuitous events and relationships. The second, more recent, program is still struggling to find the needed funds and participants to help manage several local colonies.

Organization 1

This organization was started in 1992 in a small coastal town in New England that has a large tourist trade. When visitors complained to local shopkeepers and the chamber of commerce about the poor health of the cats living on the waterfront, the president of the chamber of commerce and two women who had been rescuing and feeding cats for years decided to obtain the support of the chamber to work with local restaurants to improve the situation. A local veterinarian, also a member of the chamber, offered to sterilize the first twenty-five cats free of charge. A formal program for feral cats, with organized feeding schedules and local veterinary support, was created.

Group members soon discovered that many tame cats and kittens beyond the waterfront also had no place to call home. Although one experienced cat caretaker initially offered to shelter the cats, problems with infectious diseases arose and the need for a larger space became apparent. Shelters in nearby towns were open-admission and already had more cats than they could handle. The group began raising funds for a limited admission, cats-only shelter. The shelter has been very successful: in its first five years, it placed 3,500 cats. More than 400 cats have been trapped in the town and surrounding area. In the summer of 1998, only a single litter of three kittens was born on the waterfront—to a cat the group had been unable to trap. About 35 feral cats still live in the city, and about 75 more live in the surrounding area. Long-time residents say that cats and kittens used to be everywhere but are now under control. This program has been so successful that the waterfront feral cats are now dying of old age.

This extremely successful program had the right combination of people and support including the following: (1) credibility for the organization from the chamber of commerce; (2) publicity, pictures in the daily news, and a free spot for the cat of the week in the local newspaper, which improved adoptions; (3) aggressive, experienced fund raisers using mailings, donation cans, adoption fees, and fund-raising events; (4) links to businesses, the press, lawyers, and others with special skills, particularly those who serve on its board; (5) health department and animal care and control support; (6) lots of volunteers, many with cat care or trapping expertise; (7) veterinary support in terms of services provided (including spaying and neutering kittens as young as eight weeks old) and public support; (8) paid shelter staff, including a manager; and (9) an executive board whose members have excellent organizational skills, financial resources, connections, and feral cat expertise.

The group has continued to create new programs—from feral cat managed colonies and a shelter to school programs, a video tape, and cat visitation programs—with more plans for the future.

Organization 2

This program began in spring of 1997 when the head of a cat rescue group in a Massachusetts bedroom community called a meeting in town to address the feral cat problem. The town, which has no real industry and a rather apathetic view of pet overpopulation, did not have a local shelter. The animal control agency is dog-oriented. Several cat rescue group members had been feeding and placing cats for a number of years and owned several cats themselves. One of them had noticed cats around a business property and, in looking for resources to help them, had learned about TTVAR-M. A few more people joined after the initial meeting and through word of mouth.

The group designates different members for different tasks, such as answering phone messages, filing out the paperwork for nonprofit status, trapping, adopting, fostering, organizing, fundraising, and contacting the media. The group has coalesced well and counts a range of skills, talents, and interests among the members. The group has made a serious effort to focus on its particular mission and approach it pragmatically. Its phone answering message and materials specify that it does not handle sick, injured, or socialized cats and cannot take on new colonies. As of 1999 the group was working with four caretakers and their colonies, slowly trapping and sterilizing cats and helping caretakers obtain food and build shelters for their colonies. Plans for media coverage—for fundraising and adoption—were also underway.

Unfortunately, the group has had to work with serious handicaps. There still is no local shelter. Animal control officers view themselves as dog wardens and their attitudes' toward feral cat management vary from uninterested to actively hostile. After eighteen months of operation, only three veterinarians were willing to help the group. One only performed neutering surgeries (although he also would provide other health care), and one only accepted cats by appointment. None would sterilize cats younger than four months old, nor would any ear-tip or provide some other type of identification such as a microchip or a tattoo. As a result, one all-gray cat colony has been a real challenge to trap and sterilize. There are no other groups in the area to provide support services for fostering or adoption. But the group tries to concentrate on its accomplishments.

Case Study 3: Three Veterinarians

These three veterinarians come from two different states and from different practice situations and perspectives, but all three are involved in feral and stray cats. One provides a service that caretakers can use, one deals with feral cat caretakers in a limited way and provides homes for stray cats and kittens, and one works with an established nonprofit organization.

Veterinarian 1

This veterinarian began his career as a relief veterinarian. After many years, he wanted a more stable working situation and decided to try working at a spay/neuter clinic. After a short time, it became obvious to him that there was a need for low-cost surgical sterilization. With a colleague, he started his own clinic in California. It has proven economically viable to provide low-cost services (about 60 percent less than full-service clinics) in that region, and he now owns four "wellness" clinics. The clinics average forty-five surgeries per day, some performed by himself or staff veterinarians and others performed by veterinarians interested in learning his techniques. About 60 percent of the surgeries are performed on cats, a high percentage of whom are feral. The clinics will perform prepubertal sterilization on animals as young as six weeks old. His clinic provides all veterinary care for one large campus's feral cat program and for many city cats. He is committed to providing veterinary services for feral cat caretakers and others with limited means who need preventive cat health care.

Veterinarian 2

This practitioner is limited in her ability to provide sterilization for feral cats because she is the only veterinarian in her cats-only Massachusetts practice, has a limited number of surgical packs, and has no squeeze cages. She takes in about thirty-five strays and animals from a nearby shelter annually for medical care and placement. She also participates in several of the local subsidized voucher programs. She will perform prepubertal sterilization and finds that fitting kittens into the surgery schedule is easier because they don't require an overnight fast. She does her best to encourage owners to keep their cats confined. She would like to see some more organized programs in the area; there aren't any dealing specifically with feral cats. She believes that surgeries on a large number of cats must be performed on a recurring basis to make a difference. Getting the state veterinary college's students involved would be great, but the local government doesn't receive many complaints about cats and the local animal control officer is only paid to handle dog complaints—although she does what she can for cats. The local limited-admission shelter has its hands full already.

Veterinarian 3

This veterinarian began his Massachusetts practice just before the local grass-roots group became established. He heard about its TTVAR-M program and believed that it was a good approach because it provided disease and population control. He was comfortable with returning feral cats to a colony because of the community effort to provide ongoing follow-up care for the colonies. Philosophically, he was not comfortable with a trap and euthanize policy because he believed cats are a domestic species and that feral cats deserve as good a life as possible. Area shelter staff were already overburdened with cats and taming all the feral cats simply wasn't feasible.

He has an arrangement with the local grass-roots group, and he tries to accommodate the group and its different needs. Group members contact him about cats that need care or about their trapping plans. They then agree on whether the cat needs to be seen immediately or if he or she can be brought to the clinic at a more convenient time. The local group has only the best things to say about his support—emotionally, medically, and financially. They believe his dedication to the TTVAR-M program has been effective in raising the level of care for feral cats in the area.

Appendix B

HSUS Statement on Free-Roaming Cats

The Humane Society of the United States (HSUS) believes that every community has a legal and ethical responsibility to address problems associated with free-roaming domestic cats.

Free-roaming cats—owned cats allowed to go outside as well as stray and feral cats—often are hit by cars or fall victim to disease, starvation, poisons, attacks by other animals, or mistreatment by humans. Free-roaming cats also prey on small mammals, songbirds, and other wildlife; spread zoonotic diseases such as rabies; defecate on other people's property; and cause car accidents, among other problems.

When developing approaches to address problems associated with free-roaming cats, animal care and control agencies, policy makers, public health officials, veterinarians, cat owners, and the public should recognize the following:

- CATS BELONG IN HOMES. All cats deserve loving, permanent homes with responsible caregivers who keep the cats safely confined and meet their special needs. Long-term solutions developed to respond to cat-related conflicts should foster the responsible caretaking of cats.
- CATS ELUDE SIMPLE CATEGORIZATIONS. Free-roaming cats are often referred to as either stray or feral, but these designations do not reflect the many types of outdoor cats. Free-roaming cats can be owned cats who are allowed to roam; owned cats who have become lost; previously owned cats who have been abandoned and no longer have a home; quasi-owned cats who roam freely and are fed by several residents in an area but "owned" by none of them; and so-called working cats who serve as "mousers." Almost every community also has feral cats, unsocialized cats who may be one or more generations removed from a home environment and who may subsist in a colony of similar cats living on the fringes of human existence. Because cats exhibit varying degrees of sociability, even an animal care and control professional may not immediately be able to tell the difference between a feral cat and a frightened indoor-only cat who has escaped and become lost.

- CATS ARE NOT ADEQUATELY PROTECTED BY LAWS. Domestic cats have been the nation's most popular pet since the mid-1980s, and more than 60 million now live in U.S. households. But laws and policies developed to protect and control cats have not kept pace with their status as America's preferred pet. Few communities, for example, register or license cats or require that they be confined or supervised when outdoors. Fewer still regulate feral cats.

Comprehensive Cat Control Programs

Historically, communities have responded to cat-related conflicts by using methods that rarely provide long-term solutions. For example, traditional programs to reduce feral cat populations include either live-trapping and euthanizing cats or live-trapping, sterilizing, and releasing cats so that they cannot reproduce. Neither approach, however, provides a long-term solution unless carried out in conjunction with a comprehensive cat control program. Moreover, these approaches are labor- and cost-intensive and may alienate feral cat caregivers or residents not willing to tolerate free-roaming cats in their neighborhoods.

The HSUS believes that communities must develop, implement, regularly evaluate, and update comprehensive laws, policies, and education programs about cats and cat care. These must be pragmatic approaches designed to reduce cats' suffering and also respond to cat-related conflicts, yet remain acceptable to people in the community.

Local governments must adequately fund animal care and control programs and enforce cat control ordinances, using general revenues as well as monies collected through licensing and user fees. Sufficient funds must be allocated to implement prevention programs; hire and train staff; construct or renovate animal-holding facilities; and purchase and maintain equipment to handle, house, and care for cats.

The HSUS believes that community cat care and control programs should include the following:

- Mandatory registration or licensing of cats. If a fee is charged, it should be higher for unsterilized cats than sterilized cats (a concept termed "differential licensing").
- Mandatory identification of cats. In addition to requiring that cats wear collars and tags, communities should consider implementing a back-up, permanent identification system such as microchips.
- Mandatory rabies vaccinations for all cats more than three months of age.
- Mandatory sterilization of all cats adopted from public and private animal shelters and rescue groups.
- Mandatory sterilization of all free-roaming cats.
- A mandatory minimum shelter holding period for stray cats consistent with that established for stray dogs. This policy should allow for euthanasia of suffering animals prior to completion of the holding period.

- Adequate and appropriate shelter holding space, staffing, and other resources necessary to hold stray felines for the mandatory minimum holding period.
- An ongoing public-education program that promotes responsible cat care.
- Subsidized sterilization services to encourage cat owners to sterilize their animals.

Trap-Remove-Evaluate Programs

The HSUS recognizes that, in many instances, free-roaming cats must be live-trapped and, after completion of the mandatory holding period, evaluated for adoption or euthanasia. The HSUS believes that any individual or group that initiates a trap-remove-evaluate program should:

- Before trapping, place trapping-notification signs in the area and distribute informational leaflets to residents to give owners of outdoor cats a reasonable amount of time to safely confine their cats. Signs and leaflets should also educate readers about abandonment laws and restrictions on feeding unowned cats.
- Schedule several days for live-trapping and follow humane trapping guidelines. Ensure that traps are checked frequently (ideally every two to three hours, at a minimum every eight hours) so that captured animals may be transported quickly.
- Carefully evaluate captured cats to ascertain whether they are owned or possible candidates for adoption. Give them a "calm-down" period to help distinguish between cats who are simply frightened or stressed and those who are truly unsocialized.
- Survey the area regularly to ensure that all cats have been captured. Retrap if necessary.

TTVAR-M Programs

In recent years, traditional trap, sterilize, and release programs have been supplanted by more responsibly managed programs that trap, test, vaccinate, alter, release, and monitor (TTVAR-M) free-roaming cats. The goal of any TTVAR-M program should be to stabilize and eventually eliminate the colony through attrition. If a community's animal care and control agency or other group chooses to participate in TTVAR-M programs in cooperation with feral cat caregivers, it should:

- Make sure that feral cat colony maintenance programs are consistent with cat-related laws such as mandatory shelter holding periods for stray animals and ordinances prohibiting cats from roaming at large.
- Register caregivers who are willing to devote the time and resources necessary to fulfill program goals. In cooperation with caregivers, develop uniform guidelines covering colony care and maintenance, spaying and neutering, health monitoring, census-taking, and related topics.
- Assess each area to determine whether a colony can be safely maintained. For example, colonies should not be maintained near roads with heavy traf-

fic or in areas with extreme weather conditions and insufficient shelter.

- Assess the impact of feral cats on local wildlife populations before deciding whether to return the animals to an area. Cat colonies should never be maintained on lands managed for wildlife (such as wildlife sanctuaries).
- Secure the permission of landowners and residents to maintain feral cat populations on their property.
- Assess the carrying capacity of each area to determine how many cats can be released. Carrying capacity should be based on the number of colony members, the number of caregivers, the size and nature of the area, and the available resources.
- Before trapping, place trapping-notification signs in the area and distribute informational leaflets to residents to give owners of outdoor cats a reasonable amount of time to safely confine their cats. Signs and leaflets should also educate readers about abandonment laws and restrictions on feeding unowned cats.
- Schedule several days for live-trapping and follow humane trapping guidelines. Ensure that traps are checked frequently (ideally every two to three hours, at a minimum every eight hours) so that captured animals can be transported quickly.
- Carefully evaluate captured cats to determine whether they are appropriate candidates for re-admission into the colony. Socialized cats should be removed from the colony and, if possible, placed for adoption.
- Test trapped cats for fatal infectious diseases such as feline leukemia (FeLV) and feline immunodeficiency virus (FIV). Remove from the colony any cats who test positive for FeLV, FIV, or any other chronic or debilitating disease.
- Prior to release, vaccinate cats against rabies and other common diseases or viruses for which vaccinations are available.
- Sterilize cats prior to release.
- Permanently identify animals prior to release using a microchip and/or a visible means of identification such as ear-tipping or tattooing.
- Immediately trap any new cats who enter a colony and assess them for placement or release.

Appendix C
Volume Feral Cat Trapping Primer

By Dave Pauli, Director, The Humane Society of the United States
Northern Rockies Regional Office
Copyright © 1996; 2002 by Dave Pauli. All rights reserved.

Tips and Checklist

Live-trapping socialized cats can be easy. You set a trap and bait it; the cat enters, and it is caught. But when you have to catch a colony of feral cats, you may need some extra tips and techniques. It is especially important to remember that improperly set live traps can become death traps. This feral cat capture primer covers the essential elements to a successful volume live-trapping project. These elements include but are not limited to

I. Trap Quantity and Quality
A large number of clean, prepared live traps of varying sizes and functions (single door, double door, colony).

II. Bait Acceptance, Variety, and Selection
Either a good prebaiting program or a number of known, highly acceptable baits.

III. Trap Rotation and Management
An efficient presentation and trap rotation program that maximizes the effectiveness of the traps/bait during the first forty-eight hours.

Each of these essential elements has numerous subcategories. As a primer for training volunteer trappers, this document will attempt to cover only the basic elements.

I. Trap Quantity and Quality

Buy the highest quality traps available. Tomahawk, TruCatch, and Minnesota Plastic Trap are proven brands. Avoid inexpensive consumer brands because they will cost more in the long run.

Process and prepare the traps by

a) Washing to remove factory oils and odors.

b) Rubbing with a hand to locate burrs and sharp edges; clip or file down any found.

c) Dry firing and adjusting pan tension (the procedure varies depending upon make and model).

d) Painting or camouflaging traps, especially the bottom frame.

e) Marking, tagging, or otherwise identifying the traps.

Prepare and bring a variety of sizes and shapes. For example, for feral cat work, I will place a squirrel-size trap inside a cat-size trap, then place that inside a raccoon-size trap. The result: three good cat traps in the space of one. (Squirrel traps, when properly baited and set, make great cat traps because the cat cannot lunge in them and cause nose or face rubs.) Bring double-door traps for blind sets and "crawl-unders" and round traps for culverts. Also bring odd-sized traps such as dog or turtle traps. You will probably encounter a situation or a particular animal that requires that odd-sized trap. The new plastic traps are also very nice. (Do not use solid sheet metal traps. They can become death traps during even moderate temperatures.)

Have at least one trap for every three target animals (one for each is better) because you will want to saturate the site and catch the majority of animals before "trap/bait" shyness syndrome sets in.

Leave damaged and bent traps with protruding wires or edges at home. Humane treatment of captured animals is a priority and any damaged trap will inflict injury.

II. Bait Acceptance, Variety, and Selection

For this discussion, "baits" include food baits, sight attractors, gland lures, curiosity lures, electronic baits, and worry toys.

Key points include

- All animals are individuals. Most colony cats will eat any cat food, but some will prefer fish baits, some will prefer liver baits, and some will be suspicious of anything new. Offer variety.

- Match your baiting strategy to the keenest sense of your target species. For canines, use baits attractive to their sense of smell. For felines, use sight attractors or electronic squeakers; for nocturnal animals, white baits (marshmallows/eggs) work well.

- Prebaiting will greatly increase your trapping success. Often prebaiting can be done by the property owner prior to your arrival. Be sure to remove all prebaits (and other food sources) 12–20 hours before you set out a trap line. In certain situations you may want to set out traps with the doors wired open for two to three days to allow the colony to feed freely in the traps. This will allow even the most timid feral cats to become comfortable with eating from within the traps. Using quality edible bait will assist you if you have to recapture any escaped or released cats.

- Prebaiting is best accomplished in two steps. The first step is to establish accepted feeding stations for cats. Select 10–30 spots (depending on the size of the colony) that are protected from the weather, will accommodate the placement of a live trap, and will be relatively unbothered by people or dogs. When good sites are not available, you can construct them using half sheets of old plywood propped up against a building or bales of hay or straw stacked to form a tunnel. The second step is to remove or stop all other human food sources and then prebait the sites with dry food for several days. A few days before trapping begins, change the bait at the stations to canned salmon or cat food and clean the less popular stations. You can either wire open traps (preferred) during the "wet food" prebait or simply offer more attractive food.

Food baits must be fresh, edible, and attractive. A small amount of food should be placed at the front of the trap so that target animals get a taste of what is inside (or underneath) the trap. (Care should be taken not to handle the top or rear of the trap while wearing bait gloves.)

- Be creative with baits. Some of the most overlooked baits for cats are:
  water
  catnip, catnip oil
  "used" kitty litter
  cat toys
  electronic "squeakers"
  feathers
  hamster litter
  electric heating pad
- Baits can be highly species specific. Chicken eggs, marshmallows, peanut butter, catnip, fox urine, feathers, French fry trays, willow branches, gland lures, and essential oils can all be applied to attract (or repel) certain species. Fox urine, for example, can be a great "confidence builder" at a live trap for foxes, coyotes, or feral dogs. At the same time, it may repel rodents, skunks, or feral cats from entering some traps.

  Some baits, such as beaver castor or peanut butter, have universal appeal; others, such as black walnut oil or catnip, will appeal to a very select group. You want to minimize non-target species catches, so use selective baits whenever possible.
- Baits do not always have to be visible. Liquid, buried, or camouflaged baits will help minimize non-target catches of birds, such as magpies. Baits buried under the trap pan will eliminate bait theft.
- Keep your baiting strategy simple. For the average feral cat colony (30–50 cats), I will use thirty traps and four baits. I apply my basic bait plan (see below) and then adjust it to the preferences of those cats.

Bait	Percent of Traps
Host feed—generally dry cat food	35
Moist bait—canned fish/sardines	35
Specialty baits—kitty litter, catnip, water	15
No-bait, blind sets, trail sets, colony traps, family sets	15

Generally speaking, the baited sets are at the "core" or center of the colony. The specialty traps and blind sets are further away, along the cats' natural travel routes.

- Most of the truly feral cats and adult tomcats will be caught in specialty traps. They come to the colony for socialization and breeding, not for free handouts. As an example, my most productive feral tomcat trap is a double-door Tomahawk, well bedded with thick natural ground covering over the wire floor and with a slight spritz of catnip or queen-in-heat litter from shelter litter boxes.
- Scent from captured cats can be an added "bait." If one trap continues to catch cats, don't move or wash it. If you catch a dominant spraying tomcat, either leave the trap as a tomcat trap or wash it.
- Family sets work great for beavers, raccoons, and feral cats—one captured baby or young animal is transferred to a humane holding cage, and that cage is geometrically surrounded by unbaited traps.
- For winter trapping, emphasize plastic traps and try using a heating pad or disposable hand warmers with gland scent or fresh rodent droppings (pet hamster or rat) as bait. The hand warmers give off a lifelike scent that is attractive in lower temperatures. The hand warmers also can be used with catnip oil.

III. Trap Rotation and Management

Volume trapping is a supervised activity. If possible, you should remove captured animals within minutes of being caught. Good supervision and removal will minimize stress to you and the cats, increase your success rate, and make the property owner happy. Here are some basic concepts:

- Have a small team. Two to four people can handle any cat colony. Minimize activity and noise: move slowly and talk softly. Don't be shy about handing out a few treats to cats who watch you set your traps.
- Always bring plenty of hand towels and bath towels. The bath towels are used to cover the traps as they are being carried to the truck. Covering the traps calms the cats and minimizes nose rub or facial injuries. The hand towels can be used as a floor covering when you are forced to set traps on concrete.

I prefer a two-person team. When arriving at the colony, I stop at the perimeter and unload the specialty traps. I then take an hour or two to go around the perimeter and set traps along the travel paths to the colony. Trails, shelter belts, culverts, haystacks, and old outbuildings get my attention. I set blind sets, trail sets, crawl-unders, tom sets, and a few baited sets. When the team goes into the center of the colony, the feral cats will exit and be caught by these prepared sets before they become too wary or trap shy.

During this time my partner has *slowly* driven to the center of the colony, attempting to keep a written description of any cats observed. When entering the colony, my partner will slowly set the traps at the feeding stations and monitor them (too much activity will spook the colony). We try not to enter main buildings or areas that serve as dens until after I have set the perimeter traps so that the first few hours are spent catching the more socialized cats. We also want to minimize cat vocalizations, so all trapped cats are quickly covered and removed to an indoor trap transfer site.

- Design your program to be humane: Do not trap during primary pregnancy/lactation periods or during periods of extreme weather. Wire or stake any live trap set near streams or ponds.
- Always insulate the bottom of your trap with dirt, dander, straw, hay, wool cloth, or some other natural covering. Most live traps are thermally conductive and cats are fairly tactile. You want to minimize their fear of stepping on the trap floor.
- During the first two to four hours, check your traps every 15–30 minutes. This quiet activity will actually increase the curiosity of the remaining cats. After the initial period, check every hour.
- Although effective, minimize the number of traps you leave set overnight. Long capture periods increase the occurrence of nose rubs and facial injuries. Never leave any trap set overnight if the temperature will fall to 40 degrees Fahrenheit or less. Covered traps, plastic traps, and hay bale sets that offer protection from weather and predators can be left overnight. I prefer to travel the trap line one hour before dawn to reset the traps. This also serves as an "eyeball" inventory to determine how many cats are still there.
- Most feral cat colonies can be effectively controlled within forty-eight hours—but you will never have a 100 percent capture rate. There always will be a few cats who are too wild or who are traveling. You can either accept this fact or spend a lot of additional time on one or two cats.
- Trap location and placement are crucial.
  a) Location can be used to minimize nontargets. Traps on picnic tables or in trees will catch cats but not skunks.
  b) Some cats will not enter ground-set traps. Traps on building roofs, nailed to rafters, or in trees will catch these cats.
  c) Never set traps on or near the cats' community "toilet." Cats (and most people) do not like to eat in their bathroom. Set the trails to the toilet instead.
- "Trap logic" is the most difficult concept to teach. Which traps should you move? How long do you leave a "nonproductive" trap? There are no hard and fast rules. I have left some nonproductive traps for three days, and one caught a dominant tomcat on the fourth day. In general, if it is a good clean set, leave it. I like to leave the 10–15 most productive traps at the same spot and leave 5–10 of my specialty traps for the wild cats. The rest I will move around and experiment with.
- Trap Setting: The proper setting of live traps is more artistic than scientific, but here are a few basics.
  – Have the trap stable and well bedded.
  – Place some edible bait in front and some bait under the trap.
  – Make the trap floor comfortable and enticing.

- Cover and protect the trap when possible.
- Inspect, fine-tune, then dry fire (spring) the trap to make sure that everything works and that there are no door obstructions.
- Record Keeping: It is important to keep track of both traps and captured cats. Because we often set more than 100 live traps, we record the traps' positions using a global positioning system (GPS) so anyone can find them with a hand unit. We also use a trap-check form, which ensures that we do not forget to check every trap on the capture circuit. The capture form should also have a space to record information about the captured cats. If the cats are processed, either Tyvek, nylon collars, or some other marking system must be used.
- Worry Toys: Worry toys are mandatory for such species as raccoons. Worry toys are a safe item that gives the animal something to manipulate other than the trap. Cat worry toys can be balls, baits, or cat toys. They can be cardboard—like French fry containers, which are sight attractors—or plastic—like 35mm film canisters filled with applesauce. For cats, the best worry toys are catnip mice or film canisters filled with moist cat food. Both allow the cat to have something to "worry" and the canisters can provide moisture/food when chewed into. Never put metal cat food or sardine cans in a trap because they will cause tooth and foot injuries to the cats.
- Clean-up: After trapping a cat colony, most of my traps will go straight to the car wash. A few, however, may be pulled out and tagged as specialty traps. These would include those in which I had caught a dominant tomcat or a female in heat. I may save these traps "as is" if I expect to be trapping another colony within the next few weeks.

Summary

The main points to remember are to (1) have more traps than you'll need (you can borrow them from other agencies), (2) try to be smarter than your target, and (3) always minimize stress, handling, and capture time.

The most important steps of feral cat capture are completed in the 7–14 days prior to arriving at the colony. Planning and trap preparation are key elements. Consider going to the site a week before the event with a good spotlight to do an "eyeball inventory." This will give you a better estimate of the number of cats that are actually in the colony (the property owner usually overestimates). Be sure to give all trapped cats a quiet place to calm down. Never judge a cat's disposition or adoptability based on observations made while the animal is in a trap. Have enough cages or foster homes to accommodate the animals caught. Have a veterinary plan, an animal care plan, and written protocols for all stages of the event. Consider all possibilities—such as handling skunks and other nontargets, cat scratches and bites, and cat injuries to face and feet. Finally, plan, plan, plan!

Appendix D

Feral Cat Colony Tracking System

This form will help you identify and track individual cats in your colony and chart the progress of your trap-neuter-return program. Please send us a copy of your completed form(s) to help us gather statistics on feral cat colonies; this information is vital to promoting the effectiveness of nonlethal control. Use the Trap-Neuter-Return procedures as recommended in Alley Cat Allies' fact sheets.

Use One Form Per Colony

Your Name:_____

Address:_____

City: _____ State: _____ Zip: _____

Phone: _____

E-mail: _____

Caretakers' Names:

1) _____ Phone (____)_____

2) _____ Phone (____)_____

3) _____ Phone (____)_____

Name of Colony Location:
City & State:

Setting:
☐ Alley   ☐ Apartments   ☐ Offices
☐ Industrial   ☐ Park   ☐ Residential
☐ Other, describe:

Total number of cats in colony when management began:

_____ Adult Male   _____ Number of kittens homed

_____ Adult Female   _____ Number of tame cats removed

_____ Kittens   _____ Number of cats euthanized

                             _____ Number of cats remaining in managed colony

Year colony originally formed (if known):

Date current management plan was implemented:_____

Definition of *Management:* sterilize adult cats and tame and/or sterilize kittens

Has removal of this colony by euthanasia or relocation been attempted in the past? ☐ Yes ☐ No   Date of removal attempt: _____

FeLV/FIV Test used, if any: ☐ IDEXX In-house Combo SNAP   ☐ IFA (FeLV only)

Are all cats in the colony eartipped on the left ear? ☐ Yes ☐ No
If no, why not?

Veterinarian performing medical care:

_____ Phone (____)_____

Definition of *Homed:* Adopted into household.
Definition of *Relocated:* Placed in a new outside setting.

Please send a copy to: 1801 Belmont Road, NW Suite 201 Washington, DC 20009
Fax: (202) 667-3640 • www.alleycat.org

Name of Cat	1	2	3	4	5	6	7
Color							
Markings							
Sex: M/F							
Age:							
Date Trapped & By Whom:							
Surgery: N=Neuter S=Spay							
Vaccinations: R=Rabies Tag Number D=Distemper							
Parasites: Ivermectin Strongid Other?							
Eartip: =√ (left ear)							
FeLV/ FIV Test: Pos/Neg (2nd test in 30–90 days?)							
Fostered By Whom & Notes:							
R=Returned H=Homed E=Euthanized O=Other, explain							
Notes on General Health:							

Appendix E
Materials from
the Hawaiian Humane Society

Reprinted with permission from the Hawaiian Humane Society.

Feral Cat Colonies and Trap,
Neuter, Return and Manage (TNRM)

What is TNRM?

Trap, Neuter, Return, and Manage (TNRM) is a strategy to help reduce a community's population of feral cats humanely. Through the attention of dedicated, responsible caretakers, the cats are fed, sterilized, and given veterinary care so they can be kept healthy while the colony grows smaller and is eventually eliminated through natural attrition.

What is the Hawaiian Humane Society's position on TNRM?

The Humane Society supports responsible TNRM as a method to control feral cats. While the Society believes that all cats deserve a home with an owner and is working toward that end, we recognize that Hawaii has a significant number of homeless cats. Many of these cats were once socialized but have since become feral. There are many strategies to address feral cat populations, one of which is TNRM.

TNRM can be an effective strategy when responsible cat colony caretakers maintain their colonies by

- obtaining the property owner's agreement,
- ensuring colonies are in a safe environment,
- locating colonies away from protected animals,
- sterilizing all members of the colony,
- removing kittens and newly abandoned, socialized cats,
- keeping records of cats in the colonies,

- providing necessary veterinary care and microchip identification,
- ensuring that feeding areas are free of rubbish, and
- otherwise maintaining the colony so it does not become a nuisance to others.

How does the Hawaiian Humane Society support TNRM?

Since 1993 the Hawaiian Humane Society has regularly provided free sterilization surgery for feral cats in colonies managed by a caretaker. These sterilizations are made possible by donations from Humane Society members—your neighbors. Caretakers commit to provide ongoing care for the cats and are encouraged to follow guidelines for responsible colony management. The Humane Society also provides humane cat traps at no charge and offers microchip identification for feral cats for just $5.00.

How can you help?

Feeding cats in colonies isn't enough. If you are feeding stray or feral cats, please have them sterilized. Without this important step, you will soon have more mouths to feed and there will be more homeless cats in need. Call us at (808) 946-2187, ext. 285, to find out about borrowing traps and bringing cats in for surgery.

Stray cats may be lost cats. If you see a stray cat, it is important to realize that it may not be feral or abandoned—it may be someone's lost pet. If the cat is socialized enough for you to approach it or handle it, call us at (808) 946-2187, ext. 285, for advice on how you can help reunite the cat with its owner. Many cats now have microchip identification, which is not visible but can establish where the cat lives.

Care for your own cat(s). TNRM is helping reduce existing feral cat populations. To prevent new cats from adding to the problem we encourage you to

- Have all your own cats sterilized. Neuter Now is a low-cost program available to Oahu cat owners.
- Provide your cats with identification—collar and tag or microchip ID—even if they are indoor cats.
- Keep your cats safe by keeping them indoors, in a cattery, or within your yard using special cat fencing.
- Bring your cats to the Humane Society or another cat shelter if you can no longer keep them.

Additional information about TNRM is available from the Cat Friends organization at 686-2287.

Additional information on Hawaiian Humane Society programs and services is available at *www.hawaiianhumane.org*.

Neuter and Release Program
for Cat Colony Caregivers

Hawaiian Humane Society Commitment

The Hawaiian Humane Society's goal is for every cat on Oahu to have a home and a responsible owner. As we work toward that goal, we recognize the need to help cats who are currently living in colonies throughout the island. We offer this program to cat caregivers so that by working together we can end the birth of unwanted litters, find permanent homes for unwanted adult cats, and eliminate the growth of populations of unwanted cats on our island.

Cat Caregiver Responsibilities

As cat caregivers, you agree to give these cats continuous care by feeding them daily and monitoring their general health on an ongoing basis. Every attempt should be made to socialize these cats and to find them permanent homes, move them into a cattery, or bring them to the Humane Society. After surgery or when lost and returned to you, cats are to be returned to their original location. If the cats are to be released on private property, permission from the land owner should be granted so the cats will not be trapped again and turned in to the Humane Society. New cats who appear in the colony should be trapped and sterilized as soon as possible.

Cat caregivers further agree that while on Hawaiian Humane Society premises, they will

- Abide by any and all Hawaiian Humane Society rules and policies.
- Refrain from entering any restricted area.
- Refrain from disrupting the normal course of Humane Society business, including, but not limited to, interference with Receiving Desk operations.

About the Program

- This program is limited to cat caregivers who are caring for a colony of feral cats.
- Sterilization surgery will be performed free of charge.
- Owned, household cats *will not be* allowed under this program.
- In addition to the surgery, cats will be ear-notched to identify them as being sterilized. Absorbable sutures will be used so it will not be necessary to bring the cat back for suture removal.
- Cats will be examined to determine whether they are healthy enough to undergo surgery. Cat caregivers will be notified immediately if cats show overwhelming signs of disease and are not good candidates for surgery. Euthanasia of these cats will be recommended.
- Cats need to be at least 3 lbs. or 3 months old.

- A maximum of two cats per caregiver. Arrangements can be made with adequate notice—at least two days in advance—for mass appointments by e-mailing us at *hhs@hawaiianhumane.org.*
- Cat caregivers are required to sign a release prior to surgery.
- Cats *must* be brought to the Humane Society in humane animal traps. Humane animal traps make it safer to handle the cats and there is less likelihood of the cats injuring themselves or the handler. One cat per trap, please!
- All cats must be provided with one of the following identifications—collar with ID tag or microchip—to be purchased at the time of drop-off. Identification can be provided by the caregiver or purchased and applied at the Humane Society *only* when the cat is under anesthesia: collar/tag–$2.00; microchip–$5.00.
- If surgery is not performed on the same day, cats will be held overnight and caregivers will be notified. Please provide valid contact numbers.

To Schedule Surgery

- Surgery is performed seven days a week on a space available basis. Cats brought in between 6 A.M. and 8 A.M. will be sterilized the same day. Those brought in between 8 A.M. and 6 P.M. will be sterilized the following day. No surgeries are performed on holidays.
- It will no longer be necessary to make appointments for surgery.
- On the scheduled surgery date, bring cats in a humane trap to the Animal Receiving Department (on the mauka side of the building).
- You may pick up the cat the day of surgery between 5 A.M. and 9 P.M.
- To access Hawaiian Humane Society surgery schedules, please call (808) 946-2187, ext. 369. This has been designated as the Feral Cat Sterilization Helpline. Changes to schedules will also be noted on the Helpline.

Thank you for helping reduce the number of unwanted cats in our community.

(Rev. 5/01)

Neuter & Release Program Agreement For Cat Colony Caregivers

Name: _____ Date: _____

Day Phone: _____

Evening Phone: _____

Home Address: _____

City: _____ State: _____ Zip: _____

Location of cat colony/colonies: _____

_____

No. of cats currently in population: _____

How often do you visit the colony? _____

I am caring for these cats and agree to release them to their original location and provide basic care for them in the future. I understand that the following procedures will be performed on each cat:

☐ Castration or spay under injectable intramuscular anesthetic

☐ Ear-notching (R-female/L-male)

☐ Identification applied: ____microchip ____collar/tag

☐ After discussion and with prior approval by me, euthanasia if the cat is found to have severe debilitating disease

---

I agree to indemnify and hold harmless the Hawaiian Humane Society and its officers, employees, and agents from and against any and all liability arising out of any service provided.

I further agree that while on Hawaiian Humane Society premises, I will abide by any and all Hawaiian Humane Society rules and policies; refrain from entering any restricted area; and refrain from disrupting the normal course of Humane Society business, including, but not limited to, interference with Receiving Desk operations.

Signature of Cat Colony Caregiver   (Rev. 5/01)

Feral Cat Sterilization Program
Agreement for Cat Colony Caretakers

Name: _____ Date: _____

Day Phone: _____

Evening Phone: _____

Home Address: _____

City: _____ State: _____ Zip: _____

Specific location of cat colony/colonies: _____
Examples: Makiki, Kakaako Park, etc.

Number of cats currently in population: _____

By signing below, you agree to the following:

I am caring for these cats and agree to release them to their original location and provide basic care for them in the future. I understand that the following procedures will be performed on each cat:

☐ Castration or spay under injectable intramuscular anesthetic
☐ Ear-notching (R=female/L=male)
☐ Identification applied: _____microchip _____collar/tag
☐ After discussion and with prior approval by me, euthanasia if the cat is found to have severe debilitating disease

I agree to indemnify and hold harmless the Hawaiian Humane Society and its officers, employees, and agents from and against any and all liability arising out of any service provided.

I further agree that while on Hawaiian Humane Society premises, I will abide by any and all Hawaiian Humane Society rules and policies; refrain from entering any restricted area; and refrain from disrupting the normal course of Humane Society business, including, but not limited to, interference with Incoming Animals Department.

_____

Signature of Cat Colony Caregiver   Date

Hawaiian Humane Society
2700 Waialae Avenue, Honolulu, Hawaii 96826
Phone (808) 955-2187, ext. 285 • Fax (808) 955-6034

Instructions For Setting Humane Animal Traps

Push top half of trap door in; using your other hand, pull up door raising both parts to the top of the trap. On the right hand side is a trip lever (hook). Pull it towards you latching the hook to the top of the trap to hold the door up. The trap is now set.

If the trip lever becomes bent, it may be straightened with a small wrench or pliers. The end of the trip lever should be slightly angled toward the front of the trap.

Place bait in the rear of the trap.

Bait Suggestions

- For cats, mongoose or rats, use any of the following: chicken parts, tuna, canned cat food, or meats.

  Cats sometimes will not enter the trap because they do not like walking on the wire bottom. Try placing leaves or dirt over the floor of the trap, being careful not to block the quick release platform in the rear of the trap.

  When baiting the trap, make a path of bait from the front of the trap through the door and set the bulk of bait in the rear of the trap. For difficult cats, try burying the bait under the trap (directly under the quick release platform) or tying a piece of meat to the floor in the rear of the trap.

- If still not successful, try feeding the cat several nights without the trap. Then set the trap as described above.

Animal Removal

Check the trap at least once daily. If an animal is caught, place the trap in a shaded area and arrange to have the animal brought to the shelter as soon as possible.

Once an animal is trapped, cover the cage as soon as possible with a towel to provide darkness. This will help stop the animal from continuing to attempt escape and possibly injuring its nose or paws.

The shelter is open 24 hours a day to drop off a trapped animal, or you may call for our pick-up services ($10.00 fee) at (808) 946-2187, ext. 280.

If you want to release a trapped animal, slowly and carefully turn the trap on its side. Release the door lock by pushing in the top part of the door, then pull the entire door towards you and the door will open.

Please call our receiving department at (808) 946-2187, ext. 285, if you have any questions on the use of our humane traps.

Humane Animal Trap Use Agreement

Name: _____ Date: _____

Day Phone: _____

Evening Phone: (No pagers, please!) _____

Home Address: _____

City: _____ State: _____ Zip: _____

Social Security No.: _____

I agree to borrow and use the Hawaiian Humane Society's humane animal trap under the following terms and conditions:

1. This trap will be used only on premises owned or controlled by me and for trapping animals whose owners are unknown to me.
2. I will post a sign during the time that I have a trap set to warn my neighbors that a trap is in use and that their cats might be caught in this trap.
3. All trapped animals will be turned in to the Humane Society or returned to the owner if I am able to recognize the cat or if it carries identification that enables me to locate the owner.
4. The trap will not be set in such a way that the animals will be exposed to the hot sun, wind, or rain or would allow anyone to mistreat the trapped animals.
5. That the trap(s) will be returned within fourteen (14) days. If the trap(s) is not returned, I may be charged $50.00 per trap.
6. Once an animal is trapped, I will cover the trap with a towel until the animal is returned to the owner or brought in to the Humane Society. I will not transport the animal in the trunk of my car as the animal may overheat.

I, the undersigned, assume any and all liability of lawsuits that may arise in connection with the trap's use. I hold said Humane Society and its officers, agents, and employees harmless from any action, suits, or claims that may arise.

Animals may be brought to the Humane Society 24 hours a day, seven days a week. As a service to the community, we will pick up stray cats and other owned animals. If you would like an animal to be picked up, please call (808) 946-2187, ext. 280 to schedule an appointment.

_____
Signature   Date

We ask that the trap be returned by_____

_____
Signature   Actual Return Date

Number of Traps: _____Trap Number: _____

(revised 3/00)

Appendix F
Ordinance from City and County of Honolulu, Hawaii

(Article 6 of Chapter 7, which can be found at www.co.honolulu.hi.us/refs/roh/7.htm)

Article 6. Cat Identification Program

Sections:
7-6.1 Definitions.
7-6.2 Identification required.
7-6.3 Owner–Exception.
7-6.4 Removal of cat identification.
7-6.5 Cats released to the Hawaiian Humane Society.
7-6.6 Sterilization of cats.
7-6.7 Enforcement.
7-6.8 Penalty.

Sec. 7-6.1 Definitions.

For the purposes of this article:

"At large" means: (1) On the premises of a person other than an owner of the cat, without the consent of an occupant or owner of such premises, or (2) on a public street, on public or private school grounds, or in any other public place, except when under the control of an owner by leash, cord, chain, or other similar means of physical restraint that is not more than eight feet in length.

"Identification" means: (1) a collar or tag worn by a cat which includes the current name, address, and telephone number of the owner, or (2) an ear tag issued by the Hawaiian Humane Society, or (3) a microchip registering the owner with the National Computer Recovery Network or the Hawaiian Humane Society.

"Impounded cat" means any cat released to or under the custody of or control of the Hawaiian Humane Society.

"Person" includes corporations, estates, associations, partnerships and trusts, and one or more individual human beings. (Added by Ord. 95-21)

Sec. 7-6.2 Identification required.

It shall be unlawful for any person to be an owner of a cat over six months of age unless the person maintains an identification worn by the cat. This section shall not apply to cats in quarantine and cats brought into the city exclusively for the purpose of entering them in a cat show or cat exhibition and not allowed to be at large. (Added by Ord. 95-21)

Sec. 7-6.3 Owner–Exception.

"Owner" means any person owning, harboring or keeping, or providing care or sustenance for a cat, whether registered or not, or having custody of a cat, whether temporarily or permanently. This definition shall not apply to any person who has notified the Hawaiian Humane Society of the cat at large that the person has taken into possession and:

(1) Who is or will be transporting the cat to the Hawaiian Humane Society; or

(2) Who has made arrangements with the Hawaiian Humane Society to have the cat picked up by the Hawaiian Humane Society. (Added by Ord. 95-21)

Sec. 7-6.4 Removal of cat identification.

It shall be unlawful for any person other than an officer of or a person authorized by the Hawaiian Humane Society to remove any identification from any cat not owned by the person. (Added by Ord. 95-21)

Sec. 7-6.5 Cats released to the Hawaiian Humane Society.

(a) Any person who takes into the person's possession any cat at large shall immediately notify the Hawaiian Humane Society and shall release the cat to the Hawaiian Humane Society upon request.

(b) In the case of any cat released to the Hawaiian Humane Society wearing an identification, the Hawaiian Humane Society shall make a reasonable attempt to notify the owner by telephone and shall send written notice to the owner. The cat shall be held by the Hawaiian Humane Society for not less than nine days, after which time the Hawaiian Humane Society may return the cat to the person who had released the cat to the Hawaiian Humane Society, offer the cat for adoption, or euthanize the cat, if not sooner recovered by the owner. An owner wishing to recover the cat shall pay a daily impoundment fee of $2.50 for each full day, or fraction thereof, that the cat is held by the Hawaiian Humane Society.

(c) In the case of any cat released to the Hawaiian Humane Society not wearing an identification, the Hawaiian Humane Society shall hold the cat for not less than 48 hours, after which time the Hawaiian Humane Society may return the cat to the person who had released the cat to the Hawaiian Humane Society, offer the cat for adoption, or euthanize the cat, if not sooner recovered by a person claiming ownership. If a person claiming ownership seeks to recover the cat, the person shall pay a daily impoundment fee of $2.50 for each full day, or fraction thereof, that the cat is held at the Hawaiian Humane Society.

(d) Any cat released to the Hawaiian Humane Society with a "notched ear," indicative of a sterilized feral cat, shall be held at the Hawaiian Humane Society for not less than nine days, after which time the Hawaiian Humane Society may return the cat to the person who had released the cat to the Hawaiian Humane Society, offer the cat for adoption, or euthanize the cat, if not sooner recovered by a person claiming ownership. If a person claiming ownership seeks to recover the cat, the person shall pay a daily impoundment fee of $2.50 for each full day, or fraction thereof, that the cat is held at the Hawaiian Humane Society.

(e) If a cat released to the Hawaiian Humane Society is not recovered by the owner, the person who had released the cat to the Hawaiian Humane Society shall have the right of first refusal for permanent custody and ownership of the cat. (Added by Ord. 95-21)

Sec. 7-6.6 Sterilization of cats.

It shall be unlawful for a cat owner to allow a cat over the age of six months to be at large unless the cat has been sterilized by a veterinarian. (Added by Ord. 95-21)

Sec. 7-6.7 Enforcement.

An impounded cat for which an identification is not maintained by an owner may not be released by the Hawaiian Humane Society to a person claiming ownership of the cat until the owner complies with the identification requirements of this article. If an impounded cat, with or without identification, has not been sterilized, the person claiming ownership may be cited by an officer of the Hawaiian Humane Society for a violation of Section 7-6.6. The penalty for violating Section 7-6.6 shall be waived upon proof of sterilization of the cat by a veterinarian furnished to the Hawaiian Humane Society within 30 days after the date the citation was issued. (Added by Ord. 95-21)

Sec. 7-6.8 Penalty.

Any person found guilty of violating any of the provisions of this article shall be fined not more than $100.00. (Added by Ord. 95-21)

Glossary

Abandoned cat: a cat who has been deliberately left behind during a move or taken to a place distant from the home and left. These cats initially are usually fairly well socialized.

Alter: to sterilize; synonymous with spay/neuter.

Caretaker/caregiver: a person who claims responsibility for a cat. Often used to refer to people who are caring for feral cats.

Castration: to remove the male cat's testicles; synonymous with neutering.

Colony: a group of three or more free-roaming cats, not including young kittens too young to reproduce.

Euthanasia: the humane death of a cat, performed by a veterinarian or other trained individual—such as a euthanasia technician at an animal shelter—using the methods approved by groups such as The HSUS.

Feral cat: a cat who is too unsocialized (wild) to be handled and placed in a typical pet home. The cat may have be born to feral parents or may be a stray or abandoned cat who has become unsocialized.

Free-roaming: a cat who is allowed to wander at will off the owner's property or who is not confined in any way; synonymous with free-ranging.

Managed feral cat colony: a colony of cats in which TTVAR-M has been or is being performed. Testing for feline leukemia (FeLV) and/or feline immunosuppressive virus (FIV) may or may not be done.

Neutering: the surgical removal of the testicles in male cats, rendering them sterile. Can also be used to refer to either male or female surgeries. Synonymous with sterilization.

Owner: a person who claims some level of responsibility for or connection with a cat, generally tame and socialized.

Socialized: a cat who is not afraid of people, particularly in a familiar environment; often used synonymously with tame.

Spaying: the surgical removal of the female reproductive tract, including the ovaries and the uterus (womb).

Sterilization: the general term for spaying or neutering pets so that they are unable to reproduce.

Sterilization, low-cost: surgery performed at an actual cost low enough to be affordable to a large percentage of the local population, i.e., if a surgery costs the owner/caretaker $30 and it costs the veterinarian $25, then it is a low-cost spay or neuter. Commonly used incorrectly to refer to inexpensive surgeries.

Sterilization, subsidized: spay or neuter surgery in which the difference in cost between what the caretaker/owner pays and what the surgery costs the veterinarian is paid for by someone other than the caretaker/owner to make the surgery affordable to a large percentage of the local population, i.e., if the owner/caretaker pays $10 and it costs the veterinarian $30, then the veterinarian or some other group must pay the difference. Most spays and neuters referred to as "low-cost" are actually subsidized.

Stray cat: a currently or recently owned cat lost from the home. The owner may be looking for the cat and the cat may or may not be reunited with the owner. Such a cats is usually fairly well socialized.

Tame: a typical pet cat who is friendly towards people, especially familiar ones.

Trap, neuter, and return (TNR): a general approach to controlling feral cats that includes sterilization of the cats and return to their original location. Other health care may or may not be provided and ongoing care, while usually available, may not be present.

Trap, remove, and euthanize: the opposite approach from trap, neuter, and return. Cats are euthanized after removal from the colony.

Trap, remove, and relocate: feral cats are transferred to a new colony site, usually in the country or on a farm, or may be placed into cat sanctuaries where they are confined and receive care for the rest of their lives. In rare instances, feral cats may be socialized and placed into homes.

Trap, test, vaccinate, alter, return, monitor/manage (TTVAR-M): a specific level of care under the general trap, neuter, return approach. "Test" means that cats are tested for feline leukemia (FeLV) and/or feline immunosuppressive virus (FIV). In many situations where cats are tested, positive cats are not returned to the colony. Testing is the component of TTVAR-M which is most likely to be omitted. Vaccination, at least for rabies, is required (except in Hawaii and countries that are rabies-free). Vaccination for the respiratory and distemper viruses and for feline leukemia are optional.

Vasectomy: a surgical procedure in male cats that makes them unable to fertilize a female but does not remove the testicles or alter the typical male cat behaviors.

Literature Cited

Allen, M. 1998. The cat rescuers. *ASPCA Animal Watch*, Winter: 33–35.

Alley Cat Allies. 2002a. Relocation: Guidelines for safe relocation of feral cats. *www.alleycat.org/ic_fs_relocate.html*.

Alley Cat Allies. 2002b. Taming feral kittens. *www.alleycat.org/ic_fs_taming.html*.

American Veterinary Medical Association (AVMA). 1997. *AVMA directory and resource manual*, forty-sixth edition. Schaumburg, Ill.: AVMA.

Aronsohn, M.G., and A.M. Faggella. 1993. Surgical techniques for neutering 6- to 14-week-old kittens. *Journal of the American Veterinary Medical Association* 202: 53–55.

Berkeley, E.P. 1984. Controlling feral cats. *Cat Fancy*, September: 16–19.

———. 1990. Feral cats. *Cat Fancy*, July: 20–27.

———. 2001. *Maverick cats: Encounters with feral cats*. Revised and updated. Shelburne, Vt.: New England Press.

Breitschwerdt, E.B., and D.L. Kordick. 1995. Bartonellosis. *Journal of American Veterinary Medical Association* 206: 1928–1931.

Christensen, W. 1997. Are cats getting a bad rap? *Cat Fancy*, September: 20–25.

Christiansen, B. 1998. *Save our strays: How we can end pet overpopulation and stop killing healthy cats and dogs*. Napa, Cal.: Canine Learning Center.

Cleri, D.J., J.R. Vernaleo, and L.J. Lombardi. 1997. Plague pneumonia disease caused by *Yersinia pestis*. *Seminars in Respiratory Infections* 12: 12–23.

Clifton, M. 1992. Until there are none. *The Animal's Agenda* 12: 12–19.

Coleman, J.S., and S.A. Temple. 1989. Effects of free-ranging cats on wildlife: A progress report. *Proceeding of East Wildlife Damage Control Conference* 4: 9–12.

Coman, B.J., and H. Brunner. 1972. Food habits of the feral house cat in Victoria. *Journal of Wildlife Management* 36: 848–853.

Cuffe, D.J.C., J.E. Eachus, O.F. Jackson, P.F. Neville, J. Remfry. 1983. Ear-tipping for identification of neutered feral cats. *Veterinary Record* 112: 129.

D'Amore, E., E. Falcone, L. Busani, and M. Tollis. 1997. A serological survey of feline immunodeficiency virus and *Toxoplasma gondii* in stray cats. *Veterinary Research Communications* 21: 355–359.

DeBrito, P.G., and M.L. Doffermyre. 1994. Still more on feral cats. *Journal of the American Veterinary Medical Association* 204: 1547.

Donald, R.L. 1992. Should feral cats be euthanized? *Shelter Sense*, May: 3–7.

Dubey, J.P. 1996. Strategies to reduce transmission of *Toxoplasma gondii* to animals and humans. *Veterinary Parasitology* 64: 65–70.

Dubey, J.P., and R.M. Weigel. 1996. Epidemiology of *Toxoplasma gondii* in farm ecosystems. *Journal of Eukaryotic Microbiology* 43: 124S.

Dunn, E.H., and D.L. Tessaglia. 1994. Predation of birds at feeders in winter. *Journal of Field Ornithology* 65: 8–16.

Easterly, S. 1998. Heeding the call of the wild. *Cat Fancy*, September: 37–42.

Eidson, M., J.P. Thilsted, and O.J. Rollag. 1991. Clinical, clinicopathologic, and pathologic features of plague in cats: 119 cases (1977–1988). *Journal of American Veterinary Medical Association* 199: 1191–1197.

Faggella, A.M., and M.G. Aronsohn. 1993. Anesthetic techniques for neutering 6- to 14-week-old kittens. *Journal of the American Veterinary Medical Association* 202: 56–62.

Fitzgerald, B.M. 1988. Diet of domestic cats and their impact on prey populations. In *The domestic cat: The biology of its behaviour*, eds. D.C. Turner and P. Bateson. Cambridge: Cambridge University Press.

Fitzgerald, B.M., and D.C. Turner. 2000. Hunting behavior of domestic cats and their impact on prey populations. In *The domestic cat: The biology of its behaviour*, eds. D.C. Turner and P. Bateson. Cambridge: Cambridge University Press.

Gross, E.M., G. Hoida, and T. Sadeh. 1996. Opposition to trap-sterilize-release programs for feral cats. *Journal of the American Veterinary Medical Association* 208: 1380–1381.

Handy, G.H. 2001. *Animal control management: A guide for local governments*. Washington, D.C.: International City/County Management Association.

Hadidian, J., G.R. Hodge, and J.W. Grandy, eds. 1997. *Wild neighbors: The humane approach to living with wildlife*. Golden, Colo.: Fulcrum Publishing.

Harrison, G.H. 1992. Is there a killer in your house? *National Wildlife*, October/November: 10–13.

Heerens, S. 1994. More on feral cats. *Journal of the American Veterinary Medical Association* 204: 328–329.

————————. 1996. Different viewpoints on trap-sterilize-release programs. *Journal of the American Veterinary Medical Association* 209: 33–34.

Hendrix, C.M., H.S. Bruce, N.J. Kellman, G. Harrelson, and B.F. Bruhn. 1996. Cutaneous larva migrans and enteric hookworm infections. *Journal of American Veterinary Medical Association* 209: 1763–1767.

Herron, M.A., and M.R. Herron. 1972. Vasectomy in the cat. *Modern Veterinary Practice* 53: 41–43.

Hill Jr., R.E., J.J. Zimmerman, R.W. Wills, S. Patton, and W.R. Clark. 1998. Seroprevalence of antibodies against *Toxoplasma gondii* in free-ranging mammals in Iowa. *Journal of Wildlife Diseases* 34: 811–815.

Holton, L., and B. Robinson. 1992. First feral cat survey a success! *Alley Cat Action*, Summer.

Holton, L., and P. Manzoor. 1993. Managing and controlling feral cat populations: Killing the crisis and not the animal. *Veterinary Forum*, March: 100–101.

Hugh-Jones, M.E., W.T. Hubbert, and H.V. Hagstad. 1995. *Zoonoses: Recognition, control, and prevention.* Ames: Iowa State University Press.

Hughes, J.E. 1993. Feral cats. *Journal of the American Veterinary Medical Association* 203: 1256–1257.

Jochle, W., and M. Jochle. 1993. Reproduction in a feral cat population and its control with a prolactin inhibitor, cabergoline. *Journal of Reproduction and Fertility Supplement* 47: 419–424.

Johnson, K., L. Lewellen, and J. Lewellen. 1993. *Santa Clara County's pet population.* San Jose, Cal.: National Pet Alliance.

Johnson, K., and L. Lewellen. 1995. *San Diego County: Survey and analysis of the pet population.* San Diego, Cal.: San Diego Cat Fanciers, Inc.

Kaegel, J. 1999. Cats impact wildlife. *Sunday News Leader,* July 25.

Kahler, S.C. 1996. Welfare of cats depends on humankind. *Journal of the American Veterinary Medical Association* 208: 169–171.

Kapperud, G., P.A. Jenum, B. Stray-Pedersen, K.K. Melby, A. Esdild, and J. Eng. 1996. Risk factors for *Toxoplasma gondii* infection in pregnancy: Results of a prospective case-control study in Norway. *American Journal of Epidemiology* 144: 405–412.

Kendall, T.R. 1979. Cat population control: Vasectomize dominant males. *California Veterinarian* 33: 9–12.

Krebs, J.W., J.S. Smith, C. Rupprecht, and J.E. Childs. 1998. Rabies surveillance in the United States during 1997. *Journal of the American Veterinary Medical Association* 213: 1713–1728.

Kristensen, T. 1980. Feral cat control in Denmark. *The ecology and control of feral cats.* Wheathampstead, Hertfordshire, UK: The Universities Federation for Animal Welfare.

Laundre, J. 1977. The daytime behaviour of domestic cats in a free-roaming population. *Animal Behavior* 25: 990–998.

Lopez, T. 1997. Plague: Finding ways to stop a killer. *Journal of American Veterinary Medical Association* 211: 280–281.

Luke, C. 1996. Animal shelter issues. *Journal of the American Veterinary Medical Association* 208(4): 524–527.

Mahlow, J.C., and M.R. Slater. 1996. Current issues in the control of stray and feral cats. *Journal of American Veterinary Medical Association* 209(12): 2016–2020.

Manning, A.M, and A.N. Rowan. 1998. Companion animal demographics and sterilization status: Results from a survey in four Massachusetts towns. *Anthrozoös* 5: 192–201.

McGrath, M. 1996. Domestic concern about feral cats. *Journal of the American Veterinary Medical Association* 208: 1961.

McMurry, F.B., and C.C. Sperry. 1940. Food of feral house cats in Oklahoma: A progress report. *Journal of Mammology* 21: 185–190.

Mead, C.J. 1982. Ringed birds killed by cats. *Mammal Reviews* 12: 183–186.

Miller, J. 1996. The domestic cat: Perspective on the nature and diversity of cats. *Journal of the American Veterinary Medical Association* 208: 498–505.

Mirmovitch, V. 1995. Spatial organization of urban feral cats *(felis catus)* in Jerusalem. *Wildlife Research* 22: 299–310.

Mitchell, J.C., and R.A. Beck. 1992. Free-ranging domestic cat predation on native vertebrates in rural and urban Virginia. *Virginia Journal of Science* 43: 197–207.

Nassar, R., and J.E. Mosier. 1986. Understanding the dynamics of your community's pet population. *Veterinary Medicine,* December: 1120–1125.

Nassar, R., J.E. Mosier, and L.W. Williams. 1984. Study of the feline and canine populations in the Greater Las Vegas area. *American Journal of Veterinary Research* 45: 282–287.

National Pet Owners Survey, 2000–2001. New York: American Pet Products Manufacturers Association.

Neville, P.F., and J. Remfry. 1984. Effect of neutering on two groups of feral cats. *Veterinary Record* 114: 447–450.

New, J.C., M.D. Salman, M. King, J.M. Scarlett, P.H. Kass, and J.M. Hutchison. 2000. Characteristics of shelter-relinquished animals and their owners compared with animals and their owners in U.S. pet-owning households. *Journal of Applied Animal Welfare Science* 3(3): 179–201.

Nogami, S., T. Moritomo, H. Kamata, Y. Tamura, T. Sakai, K. Nakagaki, and S. Motoyoshi. 1998. Seroprevalence against *Toxoplasma gondii* in domiciled cats in Japan. *Journal of Veterinary Medical Science* 60: 1001–1004.

Norsworthy, G.D. 1975. Alternative surgical procedures for feline birth control: Tubal ligation, vasectomy. *Feline Practice* 5: 24–27.

Olsen, C.W. 1999. Vaccination of cats against emerging and reemerging zoonotic pathogens. *Advances in Veterinary Medicine* 41: 333–346.

Olson, P. 1998. *A critical evaluation of free-roaming/unowned/feral cats in the United States: Proceedings.* Denver: American Humane Association.

Passanisi, W.C., and D.W. Macdonald. 1990. *The fate of controlled feral cat colonies.* South Mims, Herefordshire, UK: Universities Federation for Animal Welfare.

Patronek, G.J. 1996. Another viewpoint on trap-sterilize-release programs. *Journal of the American Veterinary Medical Association* 209(6): 1061–1062.

——————. 1998. Free-roaming and feral cats—their impact on wildlife and human beings. *Journal of the American Veterinary Medical Association* 212: 218–226.

Remfry, J. 1978. Control of feral cat populations by long term administration of megasterol acetate. *Veterinary Record* 103: 403–404.

——————. 1980. Strategies for control. *The ecology and control of feral cats.* Wheathampstead, Hertfordshire, UK: Universities Federation for Animal Welfare.

——————. 1996. Feral cats in the United Kingdom. *Journal of American Veterinary Medical Association* 208(4): 520–523.

Robinson, S.K. 1998. The case of the missing songbirds. *Consequences* 3: 2–15.

Rotz, L.D., J.A. Hensley, C.E. Rupprecht, and J.E. Childs. 1998. Large-scale human exposures to rabid or presumed rabid animals in the United States: 22 cases (1990–1996). *Journal of the American Veterinary Medical Association* 212: 1198–1200.

Royal Holloway College University of London. 1981. *The ecology and control of feral cats.* Wheathampstead, Hertfordshire, UK: Universities Federation for Animal Welfare. (From proceedings of a symposium, Oliphant Jackson, chairman, Royal Holloway College University of London.)

Savesky, K. 1999. Loose cats. *Animals,* March/April: 19–21, 32.

Schantz, P.M. 1994. Of worms, dogs, and human hosts: Continuing challenges for veterinarians in prevention of human disease. *Journal of American Veterinary Medical Association* 204: 1023–1028.

Serpell, J.A. 1996. Evidence for an association between pet behavior and owner attachment levels. *Applied Animal Behavior Science* 47: 49–60.

Slater, M. 2001. Understanding and controlling feral cat populations. In *Consultations in feline internal medicine,* fourth edition, ed. J. August. Philadelphia: W.B. Saunders Company.

Snapp, M., and P. Glassner. 1998. Feral cats 101. *SF/SPCA Our Animals,* Spring.

Tabor, R. 1983. *The wild life of the domestic cat.* London: Arrow Books Limited.

Tegner, H. 1976. Wild feral cats. *Wildlife* 18: 78–79.

Terborgh J. 1992. Why American songbirds are vanishing. *Scientific American,* May: 98–104.

Universities Federation for Animal Welfare (UFAW). 1995. *Feral cats: Suggestions for control.* Third edition. South Mims, Herefordshire, UK: UFAW.

Viviani, S. 1999. Saving feral cats, Roman style. *Cat Fancy,* April: 42–44.

Zaunbrecher, K.I., and R.E. Smith. 1993. Neutering of feral cats as an alternative to eradication programs. *Journal of the American Veterinary Medical Association* 203(3): 449–452.

Resources

Publications

Animal Control Management: A Guide for Local Governments. 2001. Published by the International City/County Management Association. Available from The HSUS (see *National Organizations*).

Animal Sheltering. Published bimonthly by The HSUS. Subscriptions: $11 for one year, $16 for two years. Contact *Animal Sheltering,* c/o The HSUS (see *National Organizations*), or visit *www.AnimalSheltering.org.*

Compendium of Animal Rabies Prevention and Control, 2001. Available through the National Association of State Public Health Veterinarians, c/o Suzanne R. Jenkins, VMD, MPH, Virginia Department of Health, Office of Epidemiology, P.O. Box 2448, Room 113, Richmond, VA 23218. Also available online at *www.avma.org/pubhlth/rabcont.asp.*

NACA News. Published bimonthly by the National Animal Control Association. Subscriptions: $25 per year, free for members. Contact NACA (see *National Organizations*).

Protecting Animals. Published quarterly by the American Humane Association. Subscriptions: free with AHA membership. Contact AHA (see *National Organizations*).

Shelter Pages. The "Yellow Pages" of the animal care and control field, listing products and services ranging from cat confinement systems to veterinary supplies. Cost: $7.95, free with a subscription to *Animal Sheltering* magazine. Contact The HSUS (see *National Organizations*).

National Organizations

Alley Cat Allies
1801 Belmont Rd., NW
Suite 201
Washington, DC 20009
202-667-3630
Fax: 202-667-3640
E-mail: alleycat@alleycat.org
www.alleycat.org

American Humane
    Association (AHA)
63 Inverness Dr. E.
Englewood, CO 80112
303-792-9900
E-mail: *animal@americanhu-
    mane.org*
www.americanhumane.org
www.AHAShelterCentral.org

American Veterinary Medical
    Association (AVMA)
1931 N. Meacham Rd.
Suite 100
Schaumburg, IL 60173
800-248-2862
Fax: 847-925-1329
E-mail: AVMAINFO@avma.org
www.avma.org

Cat Fanciers Association (CFA)
P.O. Box 1005
Manasquan, NJ 08736-0805
732-528-9797
Fax: 732-528-7391
E-mail: cfa@cfainc.org
www.cfainc.org

Doris Day Animal League
227 Massachusetts Ave., NE
Suite 100
Washington, DC 20002
202-546-1761
Fax: 202-546-2193
E-mail: ddal@aol.org
www.ddal.org

The Humane Society of the
    United States (HSUS)
2100 L St., NW
Washington, DC 20037
202-452-1100
Fax: 301-258-3081
E-mail: asi@hsus.org
www.hsus.org
www.AnimalSheltering.org

National Animal Control
    Association (NACA)
P.O. Box 480851
Kansas City, MO 64148
800-828-6474
E-mail: naca@interserv.com
www.nacanet.org

SPAY/USA
750 Port Washington Blvd.
Port Washington, NY 11050
800-248-SPAY
Fax: 516-767-9384
www.spayusa.org

Universities Federation
    for Animal Welfare
The Old School
Brewhouse Hill
Wheathampstead
Hertfordshire AL4 8AN
United Kingdom
Phone: 44 (0) 1582 831818
Fax: 44 (0) 1582 831414
E-mail: ufaw@ufaw.org.uk
www.ufaw.org.uk

Local and Regional Organizations

Aggie Feral Cat Alliance of
Texas
Department of Veterinary
Anatomy and Public Health
College of Veterinary Medicine
Texas A&M University
College Station, TX 77843-4458
979-862-4569
E-mail: Afcat@cvm.tamu.edu
www.cvm.tamu.edu/afcat

Animal Birth Control
Dr. Marvin Mackie
11314 W. Pico Blvd.
Los Angeles, CA 90064
310-444-3114
Fax: 310-444-1469

Cat Care Society
5985 West 11th Ave.
Lakewood, CO 80214
303-239-9690
www.catcaresociety.org

Charlotte-Mecklenburg
Police Department
Animal Control Bureau
8315 Byrum Dr.
Charlotte, NC 28217
704-336-6695
Fax: 704-336-5709

City of Cape May, New Jersey
John Queenan
Director of Animal Control
and Code Enforcement
643 Washington St.
Cape May, NJ 08204-2397
609-884-9525

Feral Cat Coalition
9528 Miramar Rd., #160
San Diego, CA 92131
619-497-1599
E-mail: rsavage@feralcat.com
www.feralcat.com

Feral Cat Spay/Neuter Program
13619 Mukilteo Speedway
Suite D-5, #122,
Lynnwood, WA 98037-1606
206-528-8125
E-mail: fcsnpquestions
@hotmail.com
www.spaycat.org

Forgotten Felines of
Sonoma County
1275 Fourth St., #366
Santa Rosa, CA 95404
707-576-7999
www.forgottenfelines.com

Forsyth County Animal Shelter
1200 Fairchild Dr.
Winston-Salem, NC 27105
336-767-6293
Fax: 336-744-5289

Fort Wayne Animal Care
and Control
Belinda Lewis
3020 Hillegas Rd.
Fort Wayne, IN 46808
E-mail: Belinda.Lewis
@ci.ft-wayne.in.us

Hawaiian Humane Society
2700 Waialae Ave.
Honolulu, HI 96826-1899
808-946-2187
www.hawaiihumane.org

Longwood Gardens
P.O. Box 501
Kennett Square, PA 19348-0501
610-388-1000
www.longwoodgardens.org

Marin Humane Society (MHS)
171 Bel Marin Keys Blvd.
Novato, CA 94949
415-883-4621
www.marin-humane.org

Merrimack River Feline
    Rescue Society
P.O. Box 1176
Newburyport, MA 01950
978-462-0760
E-mail: mrfrs@mrfrs.org
www.mrfrs.org

Neponset Valley Humane Society
P.O. Box 544
Norwood, MA 02062
508-261-9924
E-mail: nvhs@conejo.com
www.conejo.com/nvhs.html

Operation Catnip
P.O. Box 141023
Gainesville, FL 32614
352-380-0940
www.operationcatnip.com

Operation Catnip
P.O. Box 90744
Raleigh, NC 27675
919-779-7247
www.operationcatnip.org

Orange County Animal Services
2769 Americana Blvd.
Orlando, FL 32839
407-352-4390
Fax: 407-352-4388
www.onetgov.net/DEPT/GMER/
    ANIMAL/

Peninsula Humane Society
12 Airport Blvd.
San Mateo, CA 94401
650-340-7022
www.peninsulahumanesociety.org

Rocky Mountain Alley Cat Alliance
(formerly Denver Alley Cat Allies)
P.O. Box 8393
Denver, CO 80201
303-623-0765
www.catalliance.org

San Francisco SPCA (SF SPCA)
2500 16th St.
San Francisco, CA 94103-4213
415-554-3071
Fax: 415-432-7942
E-mail: publicinfo@sfspca.org
www.sfspca.org

TEAM Van
Tait's Every Animal Matters
Donna Sicuranza
Executive Director
P.O. Box 591
Westbrook, CT 06498
For information: 860-399-5569
For appointments: 888-FOR-TEAM
Fax: 860-399-4530

Wake County Animal Shelter
820 Beacon Lake Dr.
Raleigh, NC 27610
919-250-1475
www.co.wake.nc.us/animal/
    default.htm

Index